Pro mountain biker

D1530007

Pro mountain biker

The Complete Manual of Mountain Biking – Bikes, Accessories, and Techniques

Jeremy Evans and Brant Richards

Motorbooks International
Publishers & Wholesalers ®

This edition first published in 1996 by

Motorbooks International Publishers & Wholesalers

PO Box 1, 729 Prospect Avenue, Osceola, WI 54020 USA

Motorbooks International is a certified trademark, registered
with the United States Patent Office.

The information in this book is true and complete to the best
of our knowledge. All recommendations are made without
any guarantee on the part of the author or Publisher, who
also disclaim any liability incurred in connection with the use
of this data or specific details.

We recognise that some words, model names and
designations, for example, mentioned herein are the
property of the trademark holder. We use them for
identification purposes only.
This is not an official publication.

Motorbooks International books are also available at
discounts in bulk quantity for industrial or sales-promotional
use. For details write to Special Sales Manager at the
Publisher's address.

Library of Congress Cataloging-in-Publication
Data is Available

ISBN 0-7603-0206-5

A QUINTET BOOK

This book was designed and produced by
Quintet Publishing LImited
6 Blundell Street
London N7 9BH

creative director: RICHARD DEWING
designer: SIMON BALLEY
project editor: STEFANIE FOSTER
editor: KIT COPPARD
technical editor: PATRICK CARPENTER
photography: STOCKFILE, BLISS, AND PSC

Quintet Publishing would like to extend very special thanks
to Alan at Shorter Rochford Cycles in Finchley, London, and
to Grant at Condor Cycles, Grays Inn Road, London for so
generously providing material for photography.

Typeset in Great Britain by
Central Southern Typesetters, Eastbourne
Manufactured in Singapore
by Bright Arts Pte Ltd
Printed in Singapore by
Star Standard Industries (Pte) Ltd.

1 introduction

the dawn of the mountain bike

The mountain bike was born in Marin County, across the bay from San Francisco in northern California, in the early 1970s. People had been "rough-stuff riding" many years before – indeed in the early days of cycling most of the roads were as rough as today's off-road tracks and trails – but this was the first attempt to create bikes specifically for off-road conditions.

It all happened because a group of riders discovered how much fun it was to blaze down the fire-roads and tracks of 2572ft high Mount Tamalpais. Conventional road bikes with their skinny tires and fragile components couldn't stand the pounding of riding downhill at speed on these rough trails, so the riders resorted to searching out old-fashioned straight-handlebar touring bikes of the 1930s, which were strong enough and had balloon tires that were wide enough to cope with the conditions. The fact that a popular model such as the Schwinn Excelsior could weigh as much as 60lb and had only a single gear and a hub brake didn't matter, as at first all the activity was downhill and the uphill trips were made courtesy of a truck whenever possible.

early purpose-built bikes

However, a few riders attempted to ride up as well as down, and before long they owed a big debt to Gary Fisher, an experienced road-race cyclist, who is credited with being the first person to try a modern derailleur multi-gear system on one of these old bikes. He also introduced thumb-shifters and the seat-post quick release – a big help since in the early days riders would drop their saddles and stand on the pedals all the way down.

The next stage was for enthusiasts to start building modern versions of these old "clunkers," "bombers," and "cruisers," using

● above *Mountain bike racing has come a long way from the first competitive events. Gary Fisher was there at the start of mountain biking, and still continues racing to this day.*

● left *Originally a top-class junior road cyclist, Tom Ritchey brought his skill as a framebuilder to mountain biking, helping Gary Fisher to create the first custom-built mountain bikes at the end of the 1970s.*

introduction

similar frame geometry but with more sophisticated components and much lighter steel tubing, which reduced the weight to under 40lb. In 1977 Joe Breeze made the first purpose-built mountain bikes using oversize chrome-moly tubing with thin walls for lighter weight, and he was soon followed by Tom Ritchey, a recognised road racer and frame builder, who moved easily into the new world of mountain bikes.

Ritchey built one of his new bikes for Gary Fisher, and then the two men joined forces, with Gary taking care of marketing and racing and using Ritchey bikes to dominate all the earliest mountain-bike races. He held the "Repack" race record for an unbeaten five years. Later Gary handed over the racing to Joe Murray, and later still he split with Tom Ritchey to produce his own line of Fisher mountain bikes with frames that were initially made in Japan.

From those early days the basic concept of the mountain bike was progressively refined. Major weight savings were made by using new Japanese aluminum wheel rims and lightweight thin-wall, knobbly-tread tires, bringing the weight of the best mountain bikes below 30lb by the early 1980s. By that stage mountain bikes were being produced in their thousands; but while development, design, and small-scale production were centered on the United States, volume production had largely shifted to the Far East. Taiwanese factories were making frames for many of the big-name manufacturers, while the Japanese, and in particular Shimano, cornered the market in components. By the mid-1990s, however, mainland China with its low labor rates had taken over as the main center of mountain-bike production.

● right *As a result of his work in developing the sport of mountain biking, Gary Fisher and his* "clunker" were *inducted into mountain biking's official Hall of Fame.*

repack – pioneer race

"Repack" was the first major mountain-bike race, and was inaugurated in the dry season of 1979. It started at the top of the Cascades fire-road on Mount Tamalpais, dropping some 1,300 feet in 1.8 miles, with an average gradient of 14 percent (1 in 7). This steepened to as much as 20 percent (1 in 5) as the riders negotiated bare rock, gravel, stones, and plain dirt. By the time the old "clunkers" got to the bottom of the Repack, all the grease in their single-hub brakes had been burnt off by the heat generated by sustained hard braking. They immediately had to be re-packed with grease – which is how the Cascades fire-road came to change its name to the Repack Road.

Repack racing was similar to modern downhill competition. Riders went off one at a time at two-minute intervals, with the starting order staggered so that known fast riders were not sent off immediately behind novice riders, since overtaking was both dangerous and difficult on the course.

downhill record

At the height of its popularity in 1979 the Repack attracted 50 or more riders each Sunday, with Gary Fisher holding the course record of 4 minutes 22 seconds and Joe Breeze just one second behind. As the rainy season set in the racing came to an end – and it didn't get going again the next season. Mountain biking in the area had become a victim of its own popularity, with a few bikers causing problems for the Rangers of the Marin Municipal Water District. At the same time many of the sport's founding fathers such as Gary Fisher and Joe Breeze were switching over to the business side of the mountain-bike scene and were too busy to risk their necks every Sunday on the slopes.

● below *Another early frame builder, Joe Breeze is shown here with the 1993 vintage Breezer. Joe stayed with low-volume, high-quality bikes for a long time, only recently moving production of some of his frames to Taiwan for the mass market.*

a decade of development

During the 1980s mountain biking went through a period of phenomenal growth. It spread around the world, catching on in Europe like wildfire, with mountain-bike sales far eclipsing those of all other kinds of cycle.

Frames became lighter and stiffer as top-quality thin-wall steel tubes were joined by aluminum, titanium, and carbon fiber as optional materials for frame building. Componentry was updated virtually every year, with Shimano leading the way in innovations with index-linked thumb shifting, Bio-Pace chainwheels, high-performance

● a b o v e *World Champion Henrik Djernis made a dramatic switch from the Ritchey Team to the BMW-Proflex team in 1995. Henk, as he's known, had won the world championships three times with Ritchey in 1992, 1993 and 1994. In 1995 he failed to finish.*

cantilever brakes, and Rapid Fire shifters. More and more manufacturers jumped on the bandwagon, but by the end of the 1980s mountain biking had reached a watershed.

Top-end developments continued to filter down to the cheaper bikes. Toe-clips were replaced by clipless pedals which locked to the soles of the shoes, and front-suspension forks, developed from motocross bikes, were becoming accepted as one answer to riding faster downhill.

innovative suspension

All this was leading to a new and very different kind of mountain bike. By the 1990s development had turned to rear suspension as well as front, in the search for a more comfortable, faster ride on rough and rocky trails.

This concept is clearly the way forward, and it seems likely that the 1990s will prove to be the decade in which full-suspension bikes are refined to near perfection.

Mountain bikes have never been so good. By the year 2000 we can only guess where new breakthroughs will lead. There seems little doubt that the bikes to come will include many superb and very desirable creations.

the bike as an efficient tool

The modern cycle has been with us since 1884, when J. K. Starley of Coventry in Britain introduced the Rover "rear-driven safety bicycle," which replaced the hobby-horses and the fast but unstable "ordinary bicycles" in use in previous decades. When combined

● b e l o w *Front suspension has come a long way since these early Schwinn Springer forks. Rock Shox were the people behind suspension fork development in mountain biking, and the model shown here – the Mag 21SL – led the way through 1994.*

● above *The rise of suspension bikes has meant that mountain bike frames have diverged from the classic "double diamond" shape. This Evian team bike, built by Trek, has a monocoque carbon fiber front triangle and a welded aluminum rear swingarm. The suspension is controlled by an air/oil shock absorber.*

● right *Remember, it's just about having fun. No matter how long you've been riding, mountain biking is about getting out there and having a good time. You don't need the best bike on the planet to carve lines in the dirt.*

with the pneumatic tire, first patented by J. B. Dunlop of Belfast, Northern Ireland, in 1888, it gave us a cycle that was recognizably similar to the bikes we see today.

Obviously there have been big changes in 100 years. Bikes have become lighter and much easier to ride; they are also very fast and extremely efficient, so much so that bikes are now recognized as being the best converters of human energy into forward motion developed thus far. It has been estimated that a cyclist can go three times as fast as a walker on one-fifth of the energy expended, and can travel 1,600 miles for the same energy output as that produced by a gallon of gasoline burnt by a car's engine.

the bike off-road

A mountain bike differs from an ordinary bike in its ability to get you off the road, away from the cars and trucks with their noise and fumes, and onto the tracks and trails where the air is sweet, the only noise is the swish of your tires, and you're not going to get run over. Maybe that's an idealized version of what off-road cycling can be like, but the serenity you find after leaving the road can be unequalled.

Going off-road is a wonderful way to explore new country. It lets you experience the natural environment first hand in a way that can't be compared to hiking or horse-riding. It's faster and more fun than the first, and less of a hassle and usually less expensive than the second. All you have to do is get out there and enjoy it. But where you ride needs consideration because different countries have different laws and regulations as to where you can and can't go off-road.

Generally you'll find a broad network of tracks in mountain bike-friendly countries offering a wide choice of terrain. This may range from hard cinder tracks on level ground, providing easy riding for all levels of ability and commitment, to boulder-strewn goat paths which may be the only way down a steep mountainside and demand top

● left *Mountain biking gets you to places that you never would get to otherwise. Here, a racer takes a breath, while enjoying the dramatic scenery around him.*

● right *The terrain that a good mountain bike will let you ride over is impressive. And you don't just have to roll over things gently. With the right techniques you can blast over things that would cripple an ordinary bike.*

introduction

choosing the best option

The first mountain bikes of the 1970s were built to satisfy a new minority craze for riding on the car-free tracks and trails of California. No one quite knows where the name "mountain bike" came from, but it caught the public imagination to a much greater degree that the more accurate all-terrain bike (ATB) label which is still occasionally used. The mountain bike was right for its time. It looked right and sounded right; people had money to spend and wanted to get out and take some exercise; and it signalled the first big change in the design of adult bikes for more than half a century.

The first mountain bikes were heavy and rugged to cope with the rigors of rough trails. They had a sit-up position so the rider could see where he was going, and they were shod with wide, knobbly tires built to prevent punctures and grip loose surfaces. Huge sales meant that the mountain bike developed very rapidly from these humble beginnings, and competition between the bike manufacturers enforced the technical innovations that have made a top-class mountain bike of the 1990s a highly sophisticated machine which is still evolving. Today, mountain bikes can be divided into three main categories – entry level, race ready, and extreme – depending on their purpose, level of sophistication, and, of course, price.

entry-level bike

If you want to get into the sport and not get burnt, then you've got to get a certain level of equipment. There are a host of look-alike bikes on the market that pretend to be mountain bikes, but actually aren't. These are called Hybrids, and whilst they're fine if you want to ride around town and look like you ride a mountain bike, they won't actually be any use if you go off-road.

To get off-road you need a bike with 26-in wheels. Hybrids use 700-C wheels, which

● above *Mountain bike racing has many disciplines, and this, Dual Slalom, is one of them. Riders race down a marked course, in pairs, weaving between the flags. First to the bottom wins. It's a great spectator event. Why? Lots of crashes!*

physical fitness, excellent technique, and steady nerves. In between these extremes there may be hard-packed dirt tracks in summer, which are transformed into swampy mud in wintertime. It is one of the wonders of modern mountain bikes that they are capable of dealing with such diverse environments.

are weaker and offer a much smaller selection of tires for off-road use. Other essentials include a triple chainset, cantilever type brakes, handlebar operated gear levers, and straight handlebars.

Anything other than this collection of features, it's not a mountain bike. Forget machines with calliper brakes, single chainrings, or whatever else there is out there.

Expect to pay around $350 for a new model, and about half that for a used secondhand bike.

race ready

As a general principle the best mountain bikes are the lightest ones. Modern high-performance mountain bikes are designed to be light and nimble, without sacrificing the frame strength and stiffness that is vital to withstand the pounding of riding or racing

● above *This is a typical entry level bike. Nothing fancy about it, just a good, regular steel frame, chunky tires, and componentry from a reliable manufacturer, such as Shimano.*

● above *The race-ready bike has frame and components of a high quality. Hi-tech materials can be used in the main frame, in this case aluminum. Everything about the bike looks faster, from the narrower seat to the more aggressive position of the bar and stem.*

off-road. With widespread use of aluminum and sometimes titanium, or occasionally carbon fiber frames at the top end of the market, all-up weights may be as little as 20lb, with money being sacrificed on the lightest group-sets and other fittings to complement the top-quality frames.

The riding position of the race-ready mountain bike is considerably flatter than that of the entry-level bike, but even with the basic refinement of bar-ends attached to the handlebars to give the rider a stretched position it is still more upright than that of a drop-handlebar road bike since it is vital for the rider to watch the trail ahead.

extreme

The sky is not far off the limit when it comes to refinements and gizmos for the extreme rider. The most obvious include the addition of bar-ends to the handlebars to give a choice of riding positions, while other refinements that are now accepted as the norm are clipless pedals that require dedicated footwear, and suspension forks, which are used by virtually all mountain-bike cross-country racers to enable them to maintain the highest possible downhill speeds on rough terrain. The present ultimate refinement for the extreme rider is the full-suspension bike. This, when combined with a monocoque (one-piece) frame, makes it look like a slimmed down motocross bike without an engine. Such ultra-sophisticated equipment can be combined with refinements such as disc and hydraulic brake systems. All in all, super-purist bikes are for those who are very serious about their sport.

getting the size right

For the enthusiast buying a mountain bike, the first basic requirement is to choose the correct frame size. Bike frames are available in sizes which are based on the distance along the seat tube from the center of the bottom bracket axle to the start of the seat post. The figure may be given in inches or centimeters. A rough method of working out which frame size is right for you is by taking your inside leg measurement (ILM) from the crotch down to the ground, when your legs are slightly apart. You then use the following formula to find the theoretical ideal frame size (IFS):

ILM x 0.65 = IFS

However, this formula gives only a very approximate figure, and getting the right size is complicated by variations in tube angles and lengths which contribute to the design of a bike and how it performs. This is particularly true of bikes that have frames which are radically different from the norm. The bottom line is that you should give a new bike as extended a trial as possible, because once you're committed to a particular frame size the only major adjustment easily available is in saddle and handlebar height,

● below *Extreme bikes often look nothing like any other bikes around. This Lotus Carbon model uses a monocoque construction to save weight, increase strength and offer unique ride characteristics. An extreme bike will be outfitted with the choicest components.*

introduction

● above *Setting up a bike to fit you is as important as getting the right bike in the first place. Set up badly, a bike can wreck your performance.*

plus a very restricted fore-or-aft adjustment of the saddle.

On a bike with a conventional horizontal top tube you should be able to straddle the tube with approximately 3–4in clearance with your feet flat on the ground. This is rather more than the norm with a road bike, but it is important as there may be painful impact between the crotch and top tube if the clearance is insufficient.

saddle-height adjustment

Once you've found your right frame size, you can fine-tune the bike to your body. Saddle height should be adjusted for efficient pedalling. The method to use is to sit on the bike and place the heel of your right foot on the right pedal, and then adjust the saddle upwards until you feel a slight stretching at the back of the knee when the pedal is in its lowest position. When the pedals and cranks are horizontal, the center of your knee joints should be vertically above the axle.

Always ensure that a sufficient length of the seatpost is left inside the seat tube, so there is no chance of the seat tube breaking under your weight as you bounce up and down along a rough track. The limited fore-and-aft adjustment of the saddle along its rails (known as "setback") can be important in fine-tuning your riding position.

● left *Women should spend extra time setting up a bike correctly, and may need to change the length of the stem on the bike or switch saddles for comfort.*

The "handlebar reach," the distance between the front of the saddle and the handlebars, is also important when choosing a bike, particularly if you have an unusually long or short upper body. For instance, women on average have a proportionally shorter body and longer legs than men, giving them a more stretched position on an average bike. On a bike this measurement is determined largely by the length of the top tube, but fine tuning is possible by saddle setback or possibly extending or reducing the stem length.

handlebar height

For general use, the bars of a mountain bike are usually set at around 1–2in below that of the saddle to give a moderately upright position with good forward vision. For racing and performance riding, however, the bars are set lower to help streamline the body and give a more aggressive riding stance in which weight can be transferred rapidly from the back to the front of the bike to cope with different terrain.

on-road riding

A tiny minority of mountain bikers are lucky enough to be able to ride exclusively off-road on tracks and trails where cars and trucks are banned. The majority of mountain bikers, however, accept that they will have to ride on macadam roads some of the time, sharing them with motorized traffic while heading for the next off-road section. The problem is that a bike is highly vulnerable if it meets an out-of-control car. Many car drivers do not appear to realize this, and drive in such a laid-back fashion with their music systems full on that they may not see a cyclist until the last moment. This can be critical in poor visibility or when a car sweeps round a tight bend.

The bottom line is that the car driver's fault is your problem. Society is inclined to shrug its shoulders when a pedestrian or cyclist is run down.

● right *Riding a mountain bike on road isn't always fun. As well as having to fight with cars for the right of the road, you've got to watch out for potholes, dogs and crazed commuters.*

off-road

The tracks, trails, and dirt roads used by mountain bikers have to be shared with walkers (often with dogs) and sometimes with horse-riders. Conflicts that lead to mountain bikes being banned from trails are usually caused by the fact that the bikes can travel so much faster. Zapping downhill at 30mph may be a lot of fun – but not if you plow into a party of hikers around the next bend. If there are other people likely to be using the trails, take it easy. Sit back, relax, enjoy the scenery, and adhere to the guidelines that follow.

● right *Before riding off-road, find out if your route is shared by pedestrians and horse-riders.*

● right Racers lead a life of crashing, thrills, and spills. Mountain bike racing gives you the chance to ride a route free from pedestrians, dogs, and horses. It doesn't mean it's always safe though. Even the best racers can crash.

● below When you're out in the wilderness a crash can put you and your bike out of action, so take care. You may be able to ride similar tracks near to home, but breaking something, either yourself or your bike, can be life threatening in the middle of nowhere.

● Ride only where you know it is legal to do so. The rules of access to off-road tracks and trails vary from country to country, but anywhere with a strong mountain-biking community will usually have plenty of terrain available.

● Other tracks may look inviting, but you should not leave the official trails: to do so may cause erosion, damage plant and animal environments, and annoy the people who have a right to be there without the presence of mountain bikers.

● Off-road tracks and dirt roads are often governed by the same laws as the highway. This means that you can be prosecuted for riding dangerously, especially if you are involved in an accident. Any form of racing is likely to be illegal, unless it is a specially organized event and permission has been obtained.

● When you meet other people, be courteous and considerate. Always slow down and give way to both walkers and horse-riders, even if it means dismounting and lifting your bike out of the way. If you are riding in a group, all riders should move to one side of the track. Be extra careful if there are children – it can be dangerous and may infuriate their parents if you ride by at speed. You should also take care to slow down for dogs – but retain the option to accelerate if they seem unfriendly! You may occasionally meet vehicles or motocross bikes which have legal access to dirt roads. They should give way to you, but do not take this for granted.

● Bikes can be almost silent, so if you are coming up on a party of hikers or horse-riders from behind give warning of your approach in as friendly a manner as possible. Bicycle bells may be unfashionable, but are useful for this kind of thing; otherwise a polite "Excuse me!," "Good morning!," or "Hello there!" will do.

● Never rip up the trails. A popular belief is that mountain bikes cause no damage to the environment. This is a fallacy, although their impact is usually considerably less than that made by horses and comes nowhere close to the damage caused by motocross machines and 4WD vehicles. A track with a hard surface

is no problem. A track with a soft surface of dirt or grass is a big problem in wet weather when it may be ripped apart by the heavy tread of mountain-bike tires. Learn to prevent skids and ride in control at all times to stop erosion. When your wheels start to carve grooves in wet ground, you will do much less damage if you get off and push or carry the bike.

● Make sure your bike is safe to ride, and will not let you down in the middle of nowhere or on a fast downhill. Learn basic maintenance and take essential spares such as a pump, tire levers, and a puncture-repair kit. In the interests of personal safety, take drink and food and wear clothing suitable for the conditions and length of the ride. Always wear a helmet. You should have at least third-party insurance cover when riding.

● Do not get lost. Carry a map or compass, as

required, and make sure you know how to use them. You should always know where you are, and have the ability to re-plan your route, cutting it short or getting down from high ground if necessary.

● Allow enough time for the ride. Getting caught by nightfall is foolhardy and potentially dangerous, particularly if the ride ends in an on-road section and you have no lights. Before you leave, work out how much time to allow, and be pessimistic. Your speed will depend on your skill, level of fitness, and the riding conditions. Tackling a route after heavy rain in mid-winter will take much longer than the same route in dry summer weather. A disused railroad line with a hard surface will be fast and easy; riding up and down big hills can be demanding, and the speed differences between riders will be greater.

● Always shut gates behind you, unless directed not to do so. When riding past farm animals, slow right down so as not to frighten or anger them. If you ride with a dog for company, keep it under control.

● Leave nothing behind except the faintest impression of your wheel tracks. Leave no litter – this includes biodegradable fruit peels and banana skins carelessly tossed onto the track. Leave no bad memories for yourself or others who are out on the same trails.

● Riding in a group should ensure some degree of safety, but groups that are bigger than three riders bring their own problems. They can put an unacceptable load on other people's enjoyment of the environment. It is no fun for a party of butterfly spotters when a dozen Grundig Series lookalikes blast through their favorite countryside.

● Riding alone has much to recommend it. You cause minimum upset to other trail users, and can set your own pace.

● Whether you ride alone or in a small group, before leaving tell someone responsible when you expect to be back and give them some idea of your route.

● a b o v e *Mountain bikers and horse riders should be allies. We're after the same access rights, after all. Frequently, though, squabbles between the two groups have led to trail access being removed. By working together and considering each other, we'll get more riding done.*

● b e l o w *Animals are unpredictable and a problem for off-road riders in many areas around the world, but unavoidable if you really get off the beaten track.*

physical injury

It doesn't happen often, but riders do occasionally fall off and knock themselves out or break a few bones in the middle of nowhere. If that happened to you, it would be nice to know that someone would come looking for you, and that they would be able to locate you before too long.

If you ride regularly it is well worth taking a course to get a First Aid certificate. A first-aid kit is of value only if someone knows how to use it, but even then the constrictions of space and weight on a bike will limit its value. Some bandages and bandaids will be enough to deal with minor cuts and abrasions, or possibly to support a fracture. In most cases injuries from falls are fairly minor, and you can keep on riding; in more serious cases it will probably be a matter of getting help as soon as possible, while caring for the injured rider:

● If two riders crash, help the worse injured first.

● If a rider is unconscious, do not leave him on his back. Use the first-aid "recovery position" to assist his breathing and cover him with a coat if possible. If a rider is unconscious and not breathing, give mouth-to-mouth resuscitation if you know how.

● Staunch any bleeding by applying a pad or hand pressure; if bleeding is in an arm or leg, raise the injured limb unless it is broken.

● Do not move the rider if he seems to be paralyzed, unless he is in immediate danger – on a road, for instance.

● Do not give the rider anything to eat, drink, or smoke.

● Do not leave the injured rider alone.

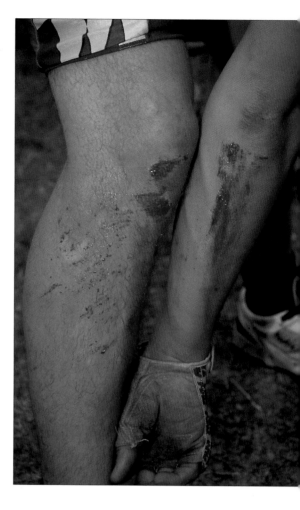

● above *Scars on the legs are still known as "road rash" throughout cycling, despite the fact they might have been acquired off-road.*

● top right *Crashing over the bars is the most common way of coming off, and it's usually the most painful. Some riders go to the trouble of learning how to crash land in a situation like this to avoid the most common downhill serious injury – the broken collarbone.*

● right *Taking it steady and enjoying the views is often the best bet. Enjoy your riding, but always take care.*

2 accessories

essential extras

handlebars and bar ends

The handlebar area includes bars, bar ends, stem and grips. It's where you work the brakes and shift gears, steer the bike, and extend the weight of your upper body. As such it demands perfect response and undergoes a great deal of stress, and everything must be in the right place with the right dimensions to suit your physique and riding style.

The handlebar area has inspired designers and engineers to produce superlight components which are nonetheless strong enough for the job. The favored material for the bars is aluminum, reinforced with butting where they pass through the stem. Optimum length has settled around 23in which is less than that on most early mountain bikes; but the bars remain virtually straight, with a choice of bar-end shapes to vary the riding position. These are mainly intended to give the rider a stretched aerodynamic position at speed, as well as allowing a much more dynamic pedalling position when hill-climbing out of the saddle.

Most bar ends have a non-slip finish which is adequate if you ride with gloves, but may slip and feel cold in the wet if you ride bare-handed. A good, thick, washable standard handlebar tape will solve any problems. It is important that the open ends of the bars have stoppers, to prevent impaling yourself on them in a crash.

● right *This is a more conventional sort of handlebar, from the manufacturer Kalloy. Mountain bike bars are built to take a great deal of pounding, but aren't indestructible. Check that your bars aren't damaged or bent. If they are, replace them.*

stems

Stems are also made in finely honed aluminum, cromoly steel, or occasionally titanium. The length and the degree of rise of the stem helps determine how stretched and low you are on the bike, and unlike your top tube is something that can easily be changed. For maximum performance a 10–20 degree rise is normal, with lengths around 4¾–6in. A rather different stem from the norm is the suspension stem of the type pioneered by Girvin. This pivots at the head-tube end, giving a minor suspension effect without the complexity, weight or expense of suspension forks. The concept is well proven, as demonstrated by Henrik Djernis who used a suspension stem with rigid forks when winning the 1993 World Mountain Bike Championship.

● left *Handlebars come in all shapes and sizes. This one has integral bar-ends to give you a multitude of climbing positions instead of just one fixed one. Always buy handlebars from a reputable company, and never ride with a bent bar.*

● above *The bar and stem area on your bike is the one that most people customize first. By switching the reach and rise and the type of handlebar, you can make your bike more comfortable.*

● l e f t *Bar ends are clampon climbing handles for mountain bikes. They allow you to get into a more aggressive and aerodynamic position, so that you can climb hills faster and cruise on the road more efficiently.*

saddles

The traditional fast shape for a high-performance saddle is the ultra-slim "turbo" style on a rigid base, with very little padding and the thin leather or synthetic covering used by road racers. It sits on aluminum or titanium rails, which are attached to the seatpost. The rails also allow the saddle to be moved a short distance forward or backwards or to be tilted for fine tuning.

● a b o v e *Mountain bike stems are made from welded tubing. This model is by Matrix, and comes as standard on Trek mountain bikes. If you're uncomfortable on your bike, changing the stem is a good way to fix it. Longer, shorter and higher stems are available.*

Whether you like the minimalist approach to saddles is a personal decision, and it always takes time for a saddle to wear in and get used to you. The minimalist saddle is certainly a hard choice for recreational biking, for which more padding and a wider tail are preferable, while a shallower central dip is more suited to the pelvic structure of women riders.

● a b o v e l e f t *This is a saddle suitable for racing or high-performance riding. Typically, it's a narrow shape allowing easy movement, and its minimal padding doesn't squish around to absorb energy. It is ideal for racing and fast riding.*

● a b o v e c e n t e r *Coming from the Italian manufacturer, Selle Italia, this Comfort model is well built with a bit more padding than the previous model. Giving a comfier ride, this is ideal for long tours or hard days in the hills.*

● a b o v e r i g h t *Women's saddles, such as this model from Avocet, are wider and shorter than men's saddles. If you're a woman riding a bike, get a woman's saddle – it'll be much more comfortable.*

Some of the most comfortable saddles are filled with a gel which redistributes itself over the base to conform with the precise shape of the rider. On the other hand, if you like hammering over hard ground, perhaps the most comfortable saddles for you are the new breed with suspension provided by springs and elastomers. These have taken up where the old-fashioned coil-spring saddles left off about 50 years ago. A typical example is the Vetta SP Suspension saddle which has an adjustable spring that allows up to ¼in of travel, with an elastomer in the main body of the saddle to cushion bumps.

seatposts

Seatposts are another item that call for the use of aluminum and titanium to produce light weight and maximum rigidity. That little tube has to support most of the weight of your body, and as a bike weaves at speed on a rocky trail it can become very highly stressed. To maintain structural integrity, it is vital to ensure there is a sufficient length of seatpost inside the seat tube when you have correctly adjusted the height. Most seatposts are marked with a maximum/minimum line which should be below seat tube level.

The seatpost is usually held in place by a clamp or binder bolt, another item which is available in superlight versions to trim yet more grams off the complete bike. It's worth keeping the lower part of the post and the clamp area lightly lubricated. This should help ensure it doesn't get permanently stuck as a result of corrosion and dirt.

Suspension seatposts are an interesting refinement that allows the saddle to travel up and down with the bumps. The lightest, and hence the best, versions use a suspension system based on doughnut-shaped elastomers. These can be mixed and matched in various grades to determine rates of springing from soft to hard, with a maximum length of travel of about 1¾in as the shaft travels up and down.

● above *Ensure when you install a seatpost that it doesn't protrude above the "Max Height" mark on the post. If the post is sticking out further than this, you could damage the post or even your frame.*

● left *This is a typical mountain bike seatpost, with a "micro adjust" cradle at the top to hold the saddle firmly. Because of its design, the saddle angle can be fine tuned to get the position just right to ensure comfort for days in the saddle.*

accessories

The advantage of a suspension seatpost is that it will cushion the ride on a rigid-tail bike when you're down on the saddle. But there is also the unavoidable fact that pedal-to-saddle length will change as the seat moves up and down. The drawbacks are weight and cost. Even the lightest suspension seatpost is heavier and more expensive than a non-suspension version, but it does represent a simple, low-cost shortcut to rear suspension on a bike.

bottles and cages

Mountain biking can be a seriously dehydrating pastime, and a rider should always carry some liquid. If the weather is wet and cold you may not need a drink, but a squirt from the water bottle can come in very handy to wash mud off your derailleur before it clogs up. The standard method of water-carrying is the bottle in a cage, which is mounted on the seat tube or down tube or both. Cages fit directly onto the frame bosses, and are usually available in aluminum rod or unbreakable plastic versions, with the aim of minimal weight. Drinking bottles are made in standard sizes up to 1¾ pints.

water carriers

There is an alternative to the traditional bottle and cage. Pioneered by CamelBak, this is worn like a backpack and contains an insulated bladder to carry liquid in full 1 or 2 liter sizes. The liquid can be chilled or hot and will stay that way for at least a short time. You drink from it by using a "bite-activated" tube that extends from the bladder to a clip that can be mounted on your shirt. The obvious advantage is that you can keep both hands on the bars during the drinking process without easing up on pedalling. In most conditions you can also be sure that the mouthpiece will stay reasonably clean since it is well above the area affected by the wheels.

Advanced models such as the CamelBak Pakster or TWP Hunchback 2 have enough space in various compartments alongside the bladder to carry spare clothes, a few snacks, some tools and maybe a mini-pump. This adds to the weight you have to carry and is also likely to increase the "hot area" of your back, but for those who like the CamelBak principle the combination pack can be an ideal compromise for wilderness touring.

basic toolset

The most basic tools you will require are a pump, a puncture-repair kit containing patches and vulcanizing glue, and two or three tire levers. In addition, all or some of the following may come in useful:

● A chain tool. This is used to drive rivets in or out when you are repairing a chain.
● Allen or hex keys. The metric system now applies universally to these tools, and 4, 5 and 6mm sizes should cover most needs.
● A small screwdriver with a Phillips head.
● A small adjustable wrench.

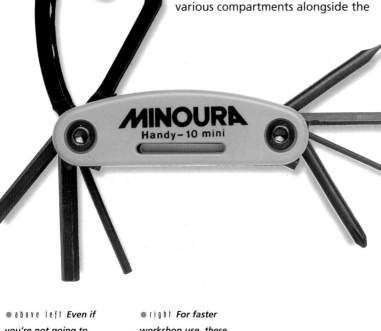

● above left *Even if you're not going to undertake major repairs on your bike, you should have access to a multi-tool such as this. It has the allen keys you require to adjust the bolts that clamp your saddle, seatpost and stem, and also allows you to tighten cables.*

● right *For faster workshop use, these three-way tools are a great choice. They are awkward to carry, though.*

accessories

Taken together, these tools could add up to a lot of bulk and weight. The best answer is likely to be to combine some or all of them in a multi-tool such as the Cool-Tool, Pocket Socket, Park Folding Multi-Tool, or the Buddy Trail Kit which contains these items and a lot more.

basic first-aid kit

If you're riding in the wilds, you should consider carrying a small first-aid kit and know how to use it and improvise with it. You don't have much space and don't want extra weight, but basic requirements can be met by:

● A selection of adhesive bandaids.

● A roll of bandage with safety pins and a small pair of scissors.

● A pad of surgical gauze.

● Antiseptic cream.

● Depending on the conditions, sunscreen and insect repellent should also be carried.

defeating thieves

A fine mountain bike is a desirable object, and it's a sad fact of modern life that thefts of these machines have soared in the early 1990s. A small number of mountain bike thieves are professionals and it can be very difficult to stop them. The majority are opportunists who can be dissuaded from taking an interest in your bike by a few simple precautions:

● Always store it indoors and out of sight at home.

● Always lock it when you temporarily park it, whether in the town or in the countryside, and lock it onto something solid. In most instances an insurance company will not pay out if an unlocked bike is stolen.

● Try to choose a well-lit public place if you have to leave it. Thieves prefer to work at their craft without spectators.

● Choose a lock that is strong enough to deter thieves. The problem is that the most secure locks are generally among the heaviest. A lightweight cable lock will deter most thieves, but an experienced operator with a suitable set of cutters will slice through it in a second. To put off such people a U-shape shackle lock is widely considered to be the best solution. This uses a hardened steel bent-shackle design which is covered in vinyl to protect the paintwork on your bike. It cannot be cut by bolt-croppers or a saw, and if the design is good it should be too difficult to drill through the locking mechanism. However, a U-lock is vulnerable to being broken open with a wedge by sheer brute force. The way to make this least possible is to fill the space in the 'U' with as many parts of the bike and what it is attached to as possible, and also to ensure it is well clear of the ground so no leverage can be applied.

● Thieves are often content to steal components rather than the whole bike. Saddles and seatposts, pumps, wheels and bags are all vulnerable and can be expensive to replace. In a high-risk area you may have to remove them when parking your bike.

mark your bike

If a stolen bike is recovered, it may be one of thousands in a police pound, many of which may be models identical to yours. Your only chance of getting it back may be fail-safe identification:

● The frame should be marked with a unique factory number, which is usually under the bottom bracket. Keep a record of it. The

● above *If you ever take your bike anywhere near a town and leave it unattended, then you'll need a good lock and a bracket to carry it with. U-locks come in many different types, but, generally, the more you spend, the better they are.*

accessories

frame can also be specially marked with your postcode and house number.

● The thief may attempt to erase any obvious markings. You can beat him by putting additional markings in hidden places, such as on the steering column inside the head tube. You can also write your name and address on a piece of paper and hide it inside the handlebars.

● You should compile a full description of your bike which can be passed to the police or insurance company if it is stolen. Useful information includes the make, model, frame number, color, group-set, bars, saddle, tires, special features, and any specific damage. A color photo will also help.

clever features. The Blackburn ToolPak, for instance, in addition to its main storage area incorporates a folding tool organizer with separate slots for tire levers, repair kit, allen keys, mini-wrench, and other items.

A saddlepack will carry only so much. If you want to carry more, such as extra clothing, food, or a camera, you will need to consider wearing a fannypack. This sits out of the way on your lower back, with a trade-off between capacity and bulk. A large, well-designed fannypack that is divided into compartments will stay comfortable and stable, but to do so it needs to include the following features:

● A waist strap which is wide enough to be

● above *Carrying equipment and food on the trail demands somewhere special, as conventional cycle race shorts don't have pockets. A fannypack makes sense and keeps things from bouncing free.*

● above right *Panniers are the way to carry large amounts of gear on a bike, but are normally only needed for extended camping trips on the road.*

basic bags

The best place to carry a bag is under the saddle. The old style of saddlebag disappeared long ago, and has been replaced by the saddlepack which fits neatly under the saddle, with Velcro straps holding it firmly to the rails and the seatpost. A small saddlepack should be just large enough to carry the vital ingredients for dealing with a puncture. Larger saddlepacks have a zipper system which allows the capacity to be expanded downwards. Any saddlepack will come in for a hard life and it's worth paying for good quality and durability. A few have particularly

comfortable, with a good buckle system. (The strap will very probably be too long, so cut off any excess.)

● Good padding, with shaped fins that fit over your hips to maintain stability.

● Compression straps to reduce the size and bulk of the bag when it is only part-filled.

touring bags

A mountain bike is the perfect answer for rough touring, giving a comfortable and safe ride in areas where road surfaces are poor and with the option of being able to follow off-road tracks and trails. With its wide tires and rugged construction a mountain bike also adapts well to being a heavy-duty luggage carrier, and has the ability to take bags with a volume totaling 5.25 cu.ft or more.

The principal requirement of a touring bike is that it should stay in balance at all speeds. This means keeping the main weight-carrying areas low down on either side of the wheel hubs, using pannier racks fitted at front and rear. These must be strongly constructed in lightweight aluminum rod, with reinforcing stays to make them rigid enough to support the stresses of loads up to about 40lb. It is possible to carry considerably more weight on a mountain bike, but safety and performance may be compromised.

The normal loading pattern is to have two larger bags of up to 1.5 cu.ft capacity mounted on the rear pannier rack. For the front rack two smaller bags of about 0.8 cu.ft are recommended. The rear bags should be mounted as far forward as possible, but must be clear of the heels of your shoes on each pedal stroke. The front bags should be mounted in the mid-wheel position. Both sets of bags will need rigid inner liners to ensure there is no interference with the spokes.

You can also carry a semi-rigid trunk bag of around 0.5 cu.ft mounted on top of the rear rack. A smaller semi-rigid handlebar bag can be used to store immediate requirements such as maps, snacks and perhaps a waterproof, though for ease of steering it is important to keep excess weight off the bar area.

All these bags should ideally be made of a waterproof material. If not you will need plastic bags or liners to protect their contents. A simple bag-to-rack locking system is necessary which makes them totally secure when on the bike, and easy to remove when required.

bells

Bells have been pushed off the roads by the noise of cars. However on tracks and trails their friendly ring can still be very useful for alerting hikers of your presence, and models such as the Trek bell and Incredibell (also available in a bar-end version) have updated the bicycle bell concept. The alternative is your own voice, or a horn which can produce a serious amount of noise. Power is usually provided by a battery, or if it's an air horn by a disposable canister. Rechargeable air horns of limited capacity, powered-up by a track pump, are available.

computers

A handlebar-mounted computer is a vital accessory if you are at all competitive, or simply like to know how fast you can go or how far you have been. Most computers have a wire connected to the sensor, but wireless computers are available which function by means of a direct signal. These make fitting

● above *Coming in all shapes and sizes, panniers can swallow enough supplies to keep you self sufficient for several days.*

accessories

slightly easier, as well as avoiding the potential problem of severing the wire if you collide with a bush.

The information from the front-wheel sensor is transmitted to the computer, which has been programmed with the exact distance the wheel will cover in one revolution. With the option of recording in kilometers or miles, it can convert this information into a number of features which are shown on the LCD display. In general terms the more features a computer boasts, the more expensive it is likely to be.

bike carriers

by car

There are three principal methods of transporting mountain bikes on your car. All these methods should allow the bikes to be securely locked to the car, discouraging theft when the vehicle is unattended.

1. On the roof. Roof-rack-mounted cycle carriers are a popular choice. The bikes are out of sight, and if you have secured them

correctly they can also be out of mind. Up to four bikes can normally be carried this way, either the right way up or upside-down, depending on the system used; some right-way-up systems require the front wheel to be removed, with the drop-outs secured to the front rack bar.

Roof-rack systems have either adjustable support clamps or purpose-designed straps to locate the bikes firmly and hold them rigid. With international standard approval, such as TUV, they are designed to withstand a great deal of stress, but should not be misused. Always ensure that the roof bars are correctly fitted to your car. Check and double-check that the bikes have been properly secured and nothing is coming loose. Moderate your driving, keeping top speed down and braking and cornering as gently as possible. Buy only a top-quality rack system which is purpose-built for carrying bicycles. Accidents caused by racks and their loads falling onto the road can have expensive and tragic consequences.

There are three main disadvantages to roof-rack bike carriers. First, you have to buy and fit roof bars. These can be expensive

• **below left** *Taking your bike by car brings about a whole new set of equipment that you need. Roof-rack mountain bike carriers are one option, but they do have the disadvantage that you have to haul the bikes up there, and they're greedy with gasoline.*

• **below right** *The best option for carrying bikes is to get them out of the wind, behind the car. Towball-mounted racks are the most solid of all, working better than the strap-on variety. A number plate and lifting board is likely to be a legal requirement.*

accessories

when designed for modern cars which lack roof gutters. If incorrectly fitted or if worn, they may damage the surrounding paintwork. Second, you have to lift the bikes up onto the roof to load them, which may be a hassle. Third, having so much clutter on the top of your car is bad news for fuel consumption.

2. Trunk carriers. This method allows bikes to be carried on the trunk of the car, with no need for special fittings. It is the most economical and in many ways the simplest carrying method.

The carrier is held to the car by a system of straps and hooks which fit around the edges of the trunk lid or tailgate. The angles of the carrier bars can be adjusted so it fits perfectly, with neoprene foam feet helping to take the load and protect your car. Support arms have space for up to two bikes, which are held securely in place by bungie cords. Once you have worked out all the adjustments, the carrier can be fitted to and taken off the car very quickly. When not in use it folds up for easy storage.

There are a number of disadvantages to trunk carriers. They can be awkward to install the first time around. If they are incorrectly installed or the hooks are worn they can damage the paintwork of your car. Some have separators on the bike arms, but you have to be careful to keep two bikes apart and ensure they don't scratch the paint off each other. When the carriers are loaded with bikes, you may not be able to open the trunk or tailgate. Most importantly, bikes carried this way may obscure the rear lights and license plate. This can be cured by mounting a secondary license plate and lighting board behind the bikes, which means your car will need to be wired for trailer lights.

3. Towball carriers. If you have a towball, the simplest and most economical bike carriers have a single or two upright V-bars on a mounting unit with cow-horn-shaped arms. This method is quick and easy and has the advantage of keeping everything well away from the paintwork of your car.

It can carry up to four bikes in an upright, side-on position, with a trailer lighting board mounted at the back. Apart from a full trailer it is probably the best method of carrying two or more bikes, though you should be aware of the length of the rack behind your car and the leverage it exerts through carrying weight so far behind the car's rear wheels.

air travel

Many airlines will carry a bike free of charge within an individual baggage allowance, which normally stands around 44lb, or within a specific number of pieces of baggage. However, on charter flights you may be charged a specific fee regardless. Check with the airline that they will be able to carry your bike back as well. Check the airline's liability for loss and damage, and the extent of your own insurance coverage.

Having confirmed that you may fly with your bike, you should check in as early as possible, and immediately tell the desk staff you are travelling with a bike. At the destination airport your bike will be carried to the baggage-collection area. Check and report any damage or loss: you will be required to fill in a claim form before leaving the area.

packed for flying

The best way to travel with a bike is to pack it in a heavy-duty cardboard box. The pedals should be removed and the handlebars turned sideways. There should be enough padding to ensure the bike is held firmly in position and that vulnerable components such as the rear derailleur cannot be damaged. These bike boxes are available direct from some major airports. Alternatively, you may prefer to buy a heavily padded, purpose-designed bike bag which is less bulky and heavy, and with a shoulder strap is much easier to carry.

lights for nights

If you go out in the dark or poor visibility, you need to see and be seen. Seeing is all about having a powerful enough front light to show you the way in safety. Being seen involves front lights, rear lights and reflective materials.

reflectors

Reflectors which pick up a vehicle's headlights are an important safety factor when riding at night on the road.

● Pedal reflectors and ankle bands are extremely effective at picking up dipped car headlights.

● Spoke-mounted wheel reflectors help a car to pick up a bike when side-on to its headlamps, but don't look good in daylight. A better system may be to use featherlight wide-angle microprism reflectors with a self-adhesive aluminum strip backing. Stuck to your wheel rims at intervals between the spokes, these give a brilliant stroboscopic effect when caught by headlights.

● Self-adhesive reflective bands or stripes can be fixed to your helmet, seat stays, forks, and other parts of your bike.

● If your clothing lacks reflective piping or panels, consider wearing a reflective belt together with wrist bands. The latter are particularly important when signalling to make a turn.

led lights

Nothing can beat an LED cycle light for being seen. These amazing devices revolutionised rear-cycle lighting when they appeared a few years ago. They are super lightweight, super compact, inexpensive, reliable, last for hundreds of hours on one set of batteries and need no replacement bulbs. They also provide a brilliant light, which can be seen at up to 2,000 feet in constant or flashing mode. The flashing mode is most visible, but in some countries, including the U.K., it is illegal to depend solely on a flashing LED for your rear lighting and a flasher must be used in conjunction with a fixed red LED or standard light. LEDs can easily be mounted anywhere and everywhere on a bike or on your body. For night-time road use we would recommend having at least two red LEDs at the rear, and a green LED facing forward mounted on your helmet.

● left and above *Pedal reflectors are some of the most effective ways of ensuring that you're seen on a bike. Because they move up-and-down, they easily catch the attention of approaching vehicles.*

standard battery lights

Conventional battery lights have all but been replaced by LEDs for use at the rear of a bike. Conventional lights are bulkier, more expensive, use considerably more battery power, and give a light that is no better than an LED but may be required as an additional light source if your LED works only in flashing mode.

At the front end of a bike conventional battery headlights are the simplest, cheapest means of seeing the way. Until recently bicycle headlights gave a poor beam, and did little more than indicate to other road users that you were there. However the new breed of lights made by firms such as Cateye, Specialized, and Vetta give a powerful clear light, using krypton and halogen bulbs of between 2.5 and 5 watts and powered by four AA or C-size batteries.

superlights

Riding off-road at night you need all the headlight power you can get, which is where the new superlights come in. These are heavyweight units for serious night-time trail riding where you need halogen lamp power of up to 20 watts and beyond. Their power comes from portable re-chargeable battery units. These are available either in the form of packs which can be hung off the top tube or fixed to your body, or as imitation "water bottles" which fit in a standard water-bottle cage. This is a neat solution, but it requires a heavy-duty cage which won't let go of that expensive bottle on a dark and bumpy downhill.

When considering power, you should also have a clear idea of how long the lamp will run before the battery is drained, and whether an auxiliary power source of standard batteries can be used to get you home. You should know exactly how the recharge system works, how long it takes, and how to maintain maximum battery life. Controls should be easy to locate and operate in the dark, with everything securely attached

so that the light will continue to work if you happen to fall off.

dressed to ride

helmets

Like having a car with all the latest safety features, it's easy to kid yourself that because you are wearing a wonderful helmet you will never crash, and that even if you do nothing bad will befall you. The truth is that a helmet has two principal advantages. First, it offers an important line of defense when you are on the road. It makes you much more visible, and alerts motorists to the fact that you are not sitting in a steel box and are vulnerable if they get too close.

Second, and this is the main item, it helps protect your head. If you are thrown off the bike and hit the top of your head on something hard, a helmet may make the

● below *Don't skimp when you're getting into mountain biking. To enjoy the sport properly, it's important to consider extra accessories like shorts, shirt, specialist shoes and, of course, a helmet.*

difference between survival and death or permanent brain damage. A cycle helmet will withstand only a certain amount of impact, however, and this may be insufficient in a road crash involving a car. However, off-road crashes commonly happen at far lower speeds, where a helmet is likely to be a brainsaver.

The structure of a cycle helmet is based on a thick layer of polystyrene foam which is approximately shaped to your head. This foam is designed to absorb the impact of a crash before your head does. In extreme cases the helmet will shatter, but sometimes the damage to the foam may not show. For this reason all manufacturers recommend that a helmet which has suffered a hard hit should be replaced regardless.

The outside of the helmet is usually covered with a thin protective layer of plastic which keeps the helmet looking neat and clean. An adjustable chin strap holds the helmet firmly in place, with anchor points at

the front and back of the helmet on both sides to help prevent it tipping back or forwards. With most helmets a good fit is achieved by trying out different thicknesses of removable Velcro-backed foam pads until the helmet feels snug.

Most helmets protect only the top of your head. However, motorcycle-style helmets which incorporate full wrap-around protection for the jaw area and a visor, such as the Bell Bellistic, are also available. These are mainly of interest to downhill racers, where the chances of crashing are much higher and the extra weight and heat of wearing such helmets is unimportant.

helmet fit

It is important that the helmet fits closely on your head without rocking backwards and forwards, and that it will stay that way if you crash.

Most helmets rely on the wearer finding the closest basic fit of the hard shell, and then experimenting with removable foam pads until the fit is tight enough all round to pull the skin of your forehead when tugged but is still comfortable. Some manufacturers have attempted to improve on this. Bell went one-up on traditional pads by introducing Reebok "Pump System" inflatable pads to give a more precise fit, while Giro attempted to tackle the problem with its Roc Loc system, which has an adjustable headband to prevent the helmet moving.

safety standards

International safety standards insure that a helmet has passed stringent tests in different countries. They are likely to include the following:

- U.S.A.: American National Standards Institute (ANSI) Z90.4; ASTM; SNELL B-90.
- U.K.: British Standard (BS) 6863.
- Australia: Australian Standard (AS) 2063.
- Germany: TUV.
- Sweden: KOVFS.

● above left *Helmets have developed a long way from the ugly brain cases of a few years ago. Now helmets are light, comfortable to wear and definitely good looking. To protect your head from crashes, you should wear one when you ride on or offroad.*

● left *Downhill riders often wear full-face helmets, to give them extra protection as they race at speeds in excess of 50mph. For this rider, his helmet has saved him from possible injury as his frame snapped in two!*

The tests are mainly based on the shock absorption of a helmet, and may also consider factors such as how the helmet is attached, whether it impairs hearing and vision, and how it copes with different weather conditions. ANSI is the most widely used standard, but it allows manufacturers to conduct their own tests. ASTM and SNELL tests are carried out independently, and the SNELL B-90 standard is widely considered the most severe, with a test in which a heavily weighted helmet is repeatedly dropped onto a metal anvil. This is administered by the non-profit-making Snell Memorial Foundation, based in the United States and with a British division. Helmets certified by Snell have to be regularly submitted for re-certification, and the Snell standard is updated at least once every five years.

shorts and tights

Getting away from Lycra or other types of stretch nylon in the world of cycling shorts and tights is difficult, because it's the most comfortable material you can wear. It fits perfectly, which is important when moving on and off the saddle; it stretches when you do; it's cool and it breathes in warm weather; and if the weather is cold it will help to keep you reasonably warm. The classic style of cycling shorts are cut with six or eight panels for a perfect fit, with elasticated thigh-grippers to prevent the legs from riding up. They should stay up at the waist on their own, but bib style shorts are available for those who prefer them. A chamois leather insert cushions the ride and protects the groin area. Modern synthetic materials are much easier to wash than the old fashioned chamois, and should be seamless with an anti-bacterial finish.

Riders who are more into mountain-bike touring may prefer to opt for hiking-style bike shorts which feature the all-important chamois insert but give a comfortable loose fit around the thighs and don't look out of place in non-cycling circles.

● below left *Obviously, colder weather calls for extra clothing. Cycling clothes are available to keep you comfortable whatever the temperature or the conditions on the trail. Breathable water-proof garments are available which don't hold in moisture and are cut to fit you as you ride.*

● below *Professional racers wear clothing emblazoned with their sponsors' logos. Fitting close to the skin, this clothing allows heat and sweat to evaporate leaving the rider cool and comfortable.*

accessories

The loose feel of these shorts may give better ventilation in hot weather, but can become a bit of a nuisance if you are moving on and off the saddle.

In cooler weather stretch-nylon tights are recommended. Some have no chamois insert and should be worn with your regular cycling shorts on the outside. The two essential features are foot stirrups and a bib top to keep the tights stretched at either end. For winter use you will need stretch-nylon tights with a nylon inner fleece (sometimes called "Roubaix" material). This keeps you warm, absorbs perspiration, and may be combined with a rain- and wind-proof outer nylon fiber.

upper body layers

Dressing for modern sports is concerned with wearing a limited number of highly effective layers. The role of the base layer is to draw away perspiration, keeping the rider cool in summer, dry in winter and warm at all times. Silk and wool are traditional materials, with lightweight polyester fleece and similar

man-made fabrics favoured by modernists. Features should include short sleeves for summer, the option of long sleeves for colder weather, a zippered neck, which helps increase ventilation, and deep back pockets on a low-cut back.

The mid-layer overlaps with the base layer (the two can in fact be interchanged). When worn over a base layer it provides extra insulation, which traps body heat and helps disperse moisture, the favored modern material being a water-resistant fleece. Features to look for include a zip at the neck, a zippered breast pocket, deep pockets in a deep back, a fairly tight fit and bright colors.

keeping out harsh weather

A top-layer jacket can be combined with the base layer or mid-layer to deal with the harshest weather. It must be able to repel wind and rain with no sweat, which means it must be "breathable." This combination becomes more difficult to achieve as the

● right *Gore-tex® is the most well known fabric that "breathes." It allows you to keep the rain out, but because of millions of tiny holes in the fabric, sweat evaporates. This allows you to keep comfortable whatever it's doing outside.*

● far right *Desert riding demands a different clothing strategy. Though it might seem like madness, covering up with 100% cotton clothing is the only way to take desert terrain. The clothes stop your skin overheating by keeping the sun's rays away.*

weather gets harsher. It may require a compromise solution, as a microfiber that is sufficiently rain-proof for a limited-duration mountain-bike ride may not be able to stand up to a long term, heavy-duty soaking. If you want to go all the way to guaranteed waterproofing, Gore-Tex® is the best-known brand name, though there are other materials which aim to do the job as well. Jackets made in these materials are expensive, and are also bulkier than a standard rain-proofed microfiber.

There are several other features to consider in a harsh-weather jacket:

● The color should be bright, so as to be seen by car drivers, with reflective piping or patches for night riding.

● Seams should be sealed with waterproof tape or welded.

● Zips should be protected by flaps, and pockets should be large enough to store gloves and perhaps a map.

● The jacket should be cut tight enough to prevent it from billowing at speed, with the front high and the back low over the saddle.

● Sleeves should have Velcro cuffs for a waterproof seal.

● The neck should draw up tight beneath the chin.

● A fold-away hood may be considered a useful option, but when wearing a helmet it is likely to be redundant.

● The jacket should be super lightweight and fold into a compact bundle for easy storage on the bike. Best of all is a jacket that is designed to fold up and convert into its own fannypack.

● Zippers under the arms and down the sides can give much needed extra ventilation.

● above left *Extreme weather calls for extreme clothing. Here a competitor in the Polaris Challenge in Britain braves the elements. Layering techniques let you do battle in all sorts of conditions.*

● above *Downhill riders wear outfits that cover all their body, often containing padding to protect themselves in the event of a crash. The padding is often the same as that used by motocross riders, as the speeds of DH racing and motocross are similar.*

hand protection

For warm-weather use, wear fingerless gloves with plenty of ventilation to prevent your hands from overheating. Check that the gloves are fully machine-washable. A combination of good palm grip and maximum shock-absorption is best achieved by materials such as single-lined neoprene or soft leather with a gel inner padding. For winter riding gloves need full-length fingers. Lining materials such as neoprene or fiberfill should keep hands and fingers warm enough for most conditions. If you plan to ride in cold, wet weather you need to check if the gloves are waterproof, as sodden gloves can lose heat rapidly.

eye protection

Eye protection is not just about style. Wearing glasses helps keep dirt and grit out of your eyes, and may save them from a sudden encounter with a branch at high speed. In cold temperatures they prevent your eyes watering, so as to ensure you can see where you are going. When the sun is shining bright they give total UV protection.

Also important is the optimum tint for the prevailing weather conditions, ranging from a coated-mirror lens for bright sun to a clear lens for overcast days. It's possible to obtain lenses in blue iridium, persimmon, clear black iridium, gray high-intensity iridium, rust, and positive-red iridium for different conditions and styles. Oakley Frogskins can be fitted with prescription lenses.

● *opposite Extreme competition riders need ultimate protection, such as in this Grundig Downhill World Cup.*

● *below Sunglasses can be bought from around $1.50, but top quality glasses specifically designed for sport cost a lot more. The reason? These eyeshades are built to withstand a shotgun blast.*

● *left For warmer riding, but still allowing protection from trail debris, this glove features ¾ length fingers. Its tough palm will stop you from skinning yourself in a crash, and the backing has cooling vents.*

● *above A top quality winter glove such as the Specialized Storm Force, should feature a water-resistant (if not waterproof) back, but retain a palm that's thin enough to allow control.*

accessories

3 advanced
technology

meeting the design challenge

Most mountain bikes are based on a diamond frame. The main exceptions are full-suspension bikes, some of which opt for more radical tube positioning. This may look good and perform well, but the conventional diamond frame is still the benchmark by which others are judged, accommodating the stresses imposed by rider and ground contact with minimum weight penalty.

● **below** *This Klein full suspension bike is one of the most radical designs around. Taking the concept of "unified rear triangle" to the maximum, it largely dispenses with classic frame construction.*

in turn is connected to the top tube.

● **Bottom Bracket.** The transverse tube for the bottom bracket is where the down tube and seat tube are connected, and where the bottom bracket axle and bearings are fitted. For general off-road use the bottom bracket should have approximately 12in ground clearance.

● **Head Tube.** This short tube plays a major structural role. It supports the front forks and handlebars, and is connected to both the top tube and the down tube. To withstand the pounding of tracks and trails, mountain bikes

● **above right** *Cannondale is an innovative company, and this Killer V model features their trademark aluminum construction, along with their radical fork.*

● **right** *Trek didn't pioneer the use of carbon fiber, but their OCLV frames have done a lot to make the material accepted. Previously, carbon had been considered unreliable and brittle. Trek changed all that with lightweight, strong, and reliable frames.*

The tubes which are joined together to make the frame are known as the "tube-set", which consists of the following components:

● **Top Tube.** The top tube extends along the top of the frame from the seat tube to the headset. Traditionally it has always been horizontal, but on mountain bikes it is often angled slightly downwards from the front to the back.

● **Seat Tube.** The seat tube extends upwards from the bottom bracket to the saddle, and directly supports the weight of the rider. The seat tube angle is measured in degrees from the horizontal.

● **Down Tube.** The down tube extends from the bottom bracket to the head tube, which

usually have oversize headsets which are wider than those found on road bikes.

● **Chain Stays & Seat Stays.** The chain and seat stays are two pairs of narrow-diameter tubes which, with the seat tube, form the rear triangle of the frame and support the rear wheel. The wheel is held in place at the hub by the rear drop-outs. The shorter the chain stays, the more rigid the rear triangle can be, allowing power to be transferred more efficiently to the back wheel. On a mountain bike there can be a serious problem with mud clogging the wheels, so it is important that the chain stays and, to a lesser extent, the seat stays give the rear wheel enough clearance on either side.

● **Bosses.** Bosses are metal fittings brazed, welded or, more rarely, glued to the frame tubes and used for mounting fittings such as brake pivots, cable guides and drink-bottle cages.

choosing the angles

Apart from the weight and stiffness of its tubes, the way a frame performs is determined by the length of the various tubes and the angles at which they are joined. For instance, a long top tube is best suited to a rider with a long body, or it may stretch him out in too flat a riding position. A frame which has a slack head-tube angle and seat-tube angle will produce a long

● a b o v e *The part of the bike most likely to affect the fit is the top tube area. Long top tubed bikes are suitable for racing and riders with long arms. Shorter top tubed bikes offer a more upright riding position.*

● l e f t *Avoid choosing a frame that has too much seatpost sticking clear of the frame. If you've got to have the post up around the "Max Height" mark, then it's too small. Likewise, having less than a couple of inches sticking out of the frame means that the bike's too big.*

● b o t t o m l e f t *The head tube of the bike gets longer (and the bars higher) the larger the frame is. Stems can be switched at point of sale to get the bike to fit you better.*

advanced technology

● top left *Despite the smooth ride that suspension gives, if you ride on smooth trails with only occasional big bumps, then there's nothing better than a rigid front end on your bike. It has no moving parts, weighs around 1.5lbs less than suspension, and comes fitted as standard!*

● centre *Kona's AA is an aluminum framed bike. Aluminum frames are renowned for their rigid ride, with an unyielding chassis ideal for extracting maximum power from the rider. They can be a little harsher through big bumps, but smooth out smaller high frequency bumps better than steel.*

● below *Specialized is at the cutting edge of suspension development, and use computer sensors to show them what's going on while their riders are plummetting down the sides of mountains.*

wheelbase which is good for a stable, fast ride on undemanding terrain, but will lack responsiveness. A frame with a more upright seat angle and head-tube angle will produce a shorter wheelbase. This enables precise handling on difficult terrain; in particular it allows good hill-climbing performance owing to better rear-wheel traction.

For a mountain bike that aspires to a reasonable level of performance, a head-tube angle of around 71 degrees has become the norm. If it is any steeper than that the steering is likely to become too twitchy; but the angle should always be selected while bearing in mind the amount the forks are raked forwards, as this also influences stability at speed. The norm for the seat-tube angle is around 74 degrees.

front forks

A conventional, rigid fork is composed of two narrow fork tubes with front drop-outs to hold the front wheel hub and bosses for the front brake. The forks are brazed or welded to the steerer tube, which fits inside the headset and is connected to the stem which holds the handlebars.

Steel is the usual fork material because it combines strength with good shock-absorbing properties. Aluminum forks are potentially lighter and give a softer ride, but they need to be oversized to withstand the stresses they are subjected to without risk of failure. (For Suspension Forks, see page 64.)

frame materials

Steel: While steel tubing is virtually the only frame material used at the cheapest end of the cycle market, it also plays a very important role in the most radical and expensive bikes in the world. Many top professional mountain-bike racers opt for steel because it can be engineered to produce the precise characteristics required by the individual rider more accurately than any other material.

The favored steel alloy for high-quality mountain-bike frame construction is chrome molybdenum (variously called chrome-moly or chromoly). It can be made into tubes which are either rolled with an almost invisible seam or drawn from a die to produce superior seamless construction. In addition the tubing may be heat treated to raise its strength and hardness, or heat "tempered" to remove its internal stresses. Both methods involve heating the tubes to high temperatures followed by cooling.

Steel has stood the test of time as a bike-frame material. It has been in regular use for over 100 years, and is available in many more varieties of tube than any alternative materials.

The principal disadvantage of steel tubing is that it is dense, which means it is heavy. However, owing to its high fatigue strength and stiffness, the best tubes can be made with wafer-thin walls. This achieves light weight while maintaining strength. In some cases steel tubing is also made "oversized". A greater tube diameter increases stiffness and strength; this allows the thickness of the tube walls to be reduced to give an overall reduction in weight.

Making thin-wall tubing is a sophisticated process, and the best steel tube-sets are expensive. A typical top-quality brand favored by mountain-bike racers among the bewildering array of tube-set trade names is Ritchey Prestige Logic. This is named after its designer, the American Tom Ritchey, who has worked closely with tube-maker Tange on mountain-bike tube-sets. Ritchey Prestige Logic is a derivative of the highly rated Tange Prestige tubing, featuring super-thin chrome molybdenum steel which is 0.5mm (0.02in) thick in the middle and 0.9mm (0.035in) thick at the butted ends, where the stresses are greatest. (Butted tubing is thickened at one end for added strength at a joint. Double-butted tubing has two changes in tube thickness, one at each end.) An additional Ritchey refinement is that

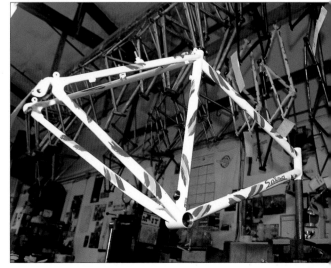

● above *Suspension forks are now a normality on high performance mountain bikes.*

● right *Just because there are high-tech materials like titanium and carbon fiber around doesn't mean that steel is a "dead" material. Builders such as Salsa continue to work in steel, producing finely crafted bikes that work well for years.*

● below *The classic steel frame has small diameter tubing that's TIG welded together. TIG is the lightest way of joining one tube to another, and it provides a strong resilient frame work. Rigid forks are precise and save weight over suspension models. Steel has much to offer. Lightweight steel bikes really ride like nothing else. A rigid set of forks with tires pumped up hard, means that the ride is fast and fun. Suspension bikes seem sluggish when you've spent the day sprinting on a steel bike.*

the butts where the frame is joined are kept very short (within the limitations demanded by TIG welding) to make the thin area of the tube as long and light as possible.

Another disadvantage of steel is that, since it is derived from iron, it has no resistance to rust when it is exposed to the atmosphere. A high-quality finish such as paint will overcome this problem. It is noticeable with many cheap mountain bikes, particularly those made for children, that the steel used is both heavy and prone to rust. These are two obvious signs of cheap tubing that has been inadequately protected with a low-quality, or poorly applied, paint finish.

Aluminum: Aluminum tubing became established as a popular material for mountain-bike frames in the early 1990s. Its big advantage is low density or light weight. In fact it is about one-third the weight of mild steel, but since steel is stiffer than aluminum by a similar factor the advantage of aluminum over a thin-wall steel tube is slight. However, aluminum also has a

considerably lower ultimate strength which, coupled with no fatigue limit, means it may break suddenly rather than deform. That is why aluminum-framed mountain bikes feature oversize tubing, which stiffens the material to the point of no flex and helps rule out any possibility of a dramatic breakage.

The lightweight, rigid platform created by oversize aluminum tubes has proved ideal for mountain bikes. Another advantage of aluminum is that in unpainted form it looks good, cannot rust, and is easy to maintain, requiring nothing more than the occasional clean with a damp cloth.

Titanium: Titanium alloy is almost as strong as steel and not quite as light as aluminum; it is fatigue-resistant and appears to have the best strength-to-weight ratio of all the frame-building metals. In addition it won't rust.

The two main disadvantages of titanium tubing are that it is difficult to assemble and very expensive. Contamination of any kind will lead to failure at the welded

joint, so the working environment during assembly must be clinically clean with an inert atmosphere. This makes it a specialized choice for both the builder and the customer, with all aspects of the complex business of titanium production and frame construction piling on the cost. The result is that you will pay a substantial premium for titanium over a top steel or aluminium frame.

AerMet: This is the trade name of a specialized steel which was first developed for military use. It claims to be the strongest metal in the world. It can be used to make wafer-thin mountain-bike tubing with a weight and strength comparable to that of titanium. Standard TIG welding is sufficient to join the tubes, rather than the more complex processes required for titanium. One disadvantage is that AerMet is extremely difficult to cut and requires specialized tools

● left *Titanium bikes were once only enjoyed by heavily walletted riders, but now thanks to mass production they're available at a kinder price.*

● bottom *Titanium tubing size-for-size is actually weaker than steel, but thankfully only two-thirds' the weight. By carefully selecting diameters, the builder can make a frame that has the ride of a steel bike, but with a big weight advantage.*

advanced technology

for the frame-building operation. AerMet can be combined with standard chrome-moly tubes when building a frame, and it is highly resistant to corrosion. Used by small-scale specialized manufacturers, it first made an appearance in the mid-1990s with bikes such as the Aermet Arrow 100. It came with a huge price tag and an unproven pedigree for mountain-bike use, but it may have the potential to become established as a standard, high-performance frame material.

Carbon fiber: Carbon fiber has also been used to make tube-sets. Its advantages are that it can be made very stiff, very light, can be built up in layers to reinforce local areas of high stress, and is corrosion-free. However, it is expensive and carbon fiber tubes are difficult to join. The joints may fail under extreme load, and because of this carbon fiber seems better suited to monocoque (single-molding) frame construction, as used on some full-suspension bikes.

● a b o v e *Offering 1in of rear wheel travel through "tuned suspension" this Lotus Carbon bike provides a smooth ride with lightweight suspension action that has no drawbacks. Its wild looks are a result of use of "clean sheet" design practices.*

● r i g h t *The experts had known all along that carbon fiber could be made into top-quality bike frames, but early attempts using tubes and lugs bonded together weren't great. Trek's Optimum Compaction Low Void technology changed all that, and finally brought carbon fiber to the masses.*

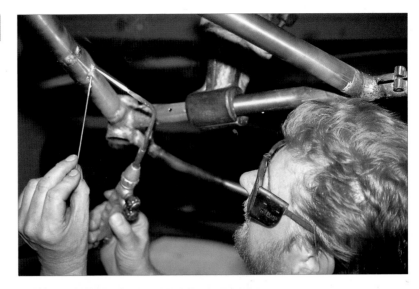

Brazing: Steel frames are traditionally joined using the method known as lugged or fillet brazing. In this process the ends of two tubes are heated and joined using a non-ferrous metal, such as brass, which has a lower melting point. In lug brazing the joint is covered by a metal collar (the lug); alternatively, the joint is made by one tube sliding into the other, which is called a fillet.

TIG welding: TIG welding is a more sophisticated, modern technique for joining metal tubes and is favored by big-scale manufacturers in Taiwan and Japan. TIG stands for "tungsten inert gas." The heat which melts the steel at the join is generated by a powerful electric current passing between the arc of the welding gun and the tube. To prevent contamination, the weld area must be protected by an inert gas such as argon. TIG welding creates a distinctive "fish-scale" head around the joint.

Bonding: Frame bonding is a specialized technique for joining tubes with epoxy resin adhesives, often using external aluminium lugs. It is used by Raleigh Special Products Division, whose Dyna-Tech range of mountain bikes features tubes made of steel, titanium, or metal-matrix composites bonded by this

● a b o v e *In the past, steel bikes were always brazed together, using a molten brass filler rod to join the tubes either in lugs, or with a lugless design. Time-consuming and needing a highly skilled operator, brazing is losing favour in mountain bike construction.*

● l e f t *Aluminum frames can't be brazed; TIG welding is the only viable option. Here Pace designer Duncan McDonald lays some beads down on an RC200 frameset. The torch belts out an electric arc which melts the metal, whilst a shield of inert argon gas protects the metal from oxidization whilst it's melted.*

● l e f t *Aluminum is an easy material to work with, far easier than steel, resulting in many builders maximizing the strength of frames by including gussets.*

advanced technology

method. Epoxy resins have powerful adhesive properties, low shrinkage, high mechanical strength, and resistance to chemical damage.

The great majority of mountain-bike frames are mass produced, with the Far East supplying the bulk of the world's production. The best of these manufacturers work to very high standards in steel, aluminum, and TIG welding, but there are still opportunities for limited production runs by custom builders, who may not be able to build frames that are any lighter or stronger than the big-league manufacturers but can hand-build to the exact requirements of individual customers – at a price.

Their main market is working to individual orders, mostly using steel tubing and traditional brazing to build made-to-measure frames. This has a decided advantage if the customer has an unusual physique, such as very long legs or a very long body, which cannot get the best out of a standard production frame. The customer discusses with the frame builder exactly what he or she wants, and can specify personal details such as the position of bosses for bottle cages or cable routes, as well as having the frame finished in any colors.

A good custom builder will be able to supply a frame which fits perfectly, has been carefully hand-assembled and finished, has all the fittings in the right places, and is an individual creation like no other mountain bike on the trail.

● below *The inside of the GT factory is typical of many bicycle construction plants around the world. Hi-tech machinery is used to measure and miter tubing, before the frames are welded together by hand. Robots aren't used, except on the cheapest of frames.*

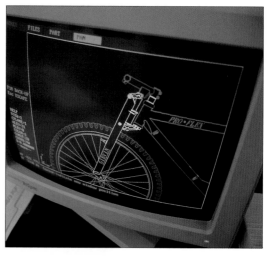

● right *Raleigh's M Trax frames use a different approach to frame construction. They are joined with high-strength aerospace adhesives. This construction lets them switch steel, titanium, or high-quality aluminum, allowing them to mix tubes within one frameset.*

● above *Modern bicycles are designed on Computer Aided Design facilities, to ensure that the bikes are ergonomic and that they're going to work well. Here designers can alter tube lengths and sizes, and even stress test the machine without having to build it.*

advanced technology

the group-set market

The majority of mountain bike group-sets are made by Shimano of Japan. Shimano successfully cornered the group-set world market during the 1980s, when it pushed out its main rivals Campagnolo (Italy) and Suntour (Japan). However, by the early 1990s the Sachs company of Germany was mounting a serious challenge to Shimano, producing innovative components and signing up big names to race for them such as Grundig champion Thomas Frischknecht and three-times world champion Hernik Djernis.

The New Success front and rear derailleurs from Sachs, as used by Team Ritchey during 1994, replaced Suntour as the only viable alternative to Shimano in derailleurs. In the same year the Sachs Power Disc hydraulic disc-brake system dominated world-class downhill events. At much the same time the American company GripShift was refining its own original twist-grips to the point where both manufacturers started to make a real dent in Shimano's hold on the mountain-bike group-set market – a dent which was enlarged by the many small manufacturers producing limited numbers of very-high-quality lightweight components such as bottom brackets, hubs, hub skewers, and brake levers.

group-set components

The principal mechanical components which are attached to a frame are known as the "group-set." Shimano produces a range of group-sets for mountain bike and road use, and many bikes are offered for sale with a choice of group-sets, such as top of the range XTR or mid-range Deore LX, at different prices. In simple terms the more you pay, the more sophisticated and lightweight the group-set components will be. Some of the components can be mixed and matched between different group-sets or with non-

Shimano components, but it is important to establish first that they are compatible. For instance, to function correctly a Dual SIS lever must be used with Dual SIS chainwheels and front derailleur.

A typical Shimano mountain-bike group-set will include the following components:

● **Rear derailleur** This is the rear gear-change mechanism, which is also known as the "rear mech." It is pulled in and out by a cable and a

● *above The rear mech has the job of hauling the chain from one sprocket to another, and taking up any chain slack that develops.*

● *below The drivetrain area of the groupset consists of the chainset, chain, front and rear mechs and the cassette cluster.*

spring, and this moves the chain across the cogs. Shimano invented the Shimano Index System (SIS) which allows each gear to shift precisely into position, one click at a time. It is standard on Shimano rear derailleurs, and also works on Dual SIS front derailleurs.

● **Front derailleur** The front gear-change mechanism is also known as the "front mech." It is pulled outwards by a spring and inwards by a cable; this moves the chain across the three chainwheels. Shimano front derailleurs are available in non-index or indexed Dual SIS modes.

● **Rear sprocket cluster** A collection of between six and eight toothed sprockets, which replaces the conventional freewheel.

● **Chainwheels** Three toothed chainwheels are mounted on the bottom bracket with crank arms attached.

● **Chain** The chain sits on the teeth of the chainwheels and rear sprocket. Mountain-bike chains suffer heavy wear, and must be regularly cleaned and replaced to avoid damaging the teeth of the rear cluster or chainwheels.

● l e f t *This is a complete set of components, in this case Shimano's STX RC. Bike manufacturers have the choice of either picking all these parts, or mixing and matching to build a complete bike.*

● **Bottom bracket** This is the central revolving spindle on which the chainwheel is mounted. Bottom brackets on early mountain bikes suffered from water and dirt getting into the bearings. Modern bottom brackets are fully sealed cassette units. They are virtually maintenance free, but may need to be completely replaced once they wear out. As well as Shimano, there is a wide choice available from specialized manufacturers using top-quality materials such as titanium.

● **Rear-wheel hub/freewheel** Shimano combines the freewheel and hub into a Freehub sealed cassette on which the rear wheel gear sprockets are mounted. It also includes a skewer and quick-release lever.

● **Front-wheel hub** The unit on which the front wheel is mounted, this includes a skewer and quick-release lever. Parallax hubs with greater torsional stiffness were introduced by Shimano for use with suspension forks. A wide range of extra-strong hubs is produced by specialized manufacturers for front and rear wheels.

● **Gear changers** Handlebar-mounted changers control the derailleur cables. Shimano gear changers are combined with the brake levers in single units and range from basic thumb shifters mounted on the top of the handlebars to the sophisticated

● l e f t *The chainset of the mountain bike is a conglomeration of three chainrings, the crankarms and a "spider" holding the rings to the crank arms. The whole thing rotates on the bottom bracket axle, which is fastened into the bottom bracket shell on the frame.*

● l e f t *Though it seems archaic and simplistic, the rear mech does its job extremely well. The tension generated in the gear cable by the thumbshifter pulls the paralellogram of the rear mech body across the sprockets, shifting the chain. Releasing the tension, a spring pulls the mech down to a smaller sprocket. Simple!*

● a b o v e *The rear sprocket cluster provides the appropriate gears according to the number of teeth.*

● l e f t *Mountain bike chain has to take all the load that you're putting through the pedals which adds up to a massive tension in low gears on steep hills. Always use the correct chain installation tool – a proper chain breaker – and be careful to follow the instructions to avoid the chain splitting under load.*

● r i g h t *The control cables that activate the gears and brakes need to be long enough so as not to ruin the frame when the bars are turned to the extreme. These casings also need to be checked periodically for cracks, so as to avoid them snapping suddenly.*

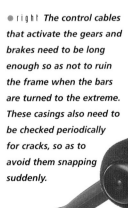

Rapid Fire Plus system. This features a two-finger shift action that allows you to push with your thumb to shift one way and pull with your forefinger to shift the other way – plus, on some models, an optical display.

● **Front and rear brakes** Powerful cantilever-style brakes with straddle wires are the popular mountain-bike choice, led by the Shimano Linear Response (SLR) system which combines brake levers, brake arches, cable housings and cables. The Shimano anti-vibration M-System claims to give similar braking performance in both wet and dry

conditions, using special brake block compounds. Disc brakes are a specialized mountain-bike option, but they are not made by Shimano.

● **Brake levers** Shimano introduced the Servo-Wave system which gives a modulated lever action, with the lever exerting progressively more force the further it is pulled. Handlebar-mounted levers to control the brake cables are integrated with the gear levers in Shimano group-sets, but the popularity of non-Shimano twist-grip gear changers has made available a wide choice of lightweight,

● right *Take time setting up your handlebar equipment to ensure that barends, brake levers and gear changes are all in the correct position.*

● above *Grip Shift units make gear changing a simple flick of the wrist, rather than a press of a button. Their simplicity and clean lines attract many riders.*

ergonomically designed brake levers built by specialized manufacturers.

● **Headset** The headset, which allows the front forks and handlebar to revolve, is sometimes sold as part of a group-set, but is often produced by specialised manufacturers.

● **Seatpost** The seatpost and its bolt are also sometimes sold as part of a group-set, but they too are often produced by specialized manufacturers using superlight metal such as titanium.

twist-grip gear changers

The move to twist-grip style gear changers for both front and rear derailleurs was made by the American company Grip Shift and by Sachs with their Power Grip. After a long period of development the twist-grip concept became so successful that by the mid-1990s many top-line mountain bikes were being fitted with twist-grips in place of the established Shimano gear shifters. Riders in the men's professional division used GripShift to win every NORBA and Grundig cross-country and downhill race in 1994.

The twist-grip concept looks good and is easily understood by any rider, but in practical terms its surge in popularity was due to a number of advantages over Shimano's top-line Rapid Fire Plus gear changers:
1. Twist-grip was considerably cheaper, whether produced by GripShift or Sachs.
2. It was also lighter, since it used primarily plastic components.
3. It was much less complex, with fewer moving parts, theoretically making it easier to maintain.

Rapid Fire Plus had a more precise shifting movement; it also left the handlebars less crowded, with more ergonomic hand-positions available and with less physical effort required to shift the gears.

● a b o v e *Shimano's STI units combine brake and shift levers. This is great as it means less weight and only one bolt to tighten. Downsides are not being able to independently adjust the angle of each component, and replacing one part means replacing both.*

● b e l o w *Disc brakes have been coming into mountain biking over the last few years, and now there are systems on the market that work well enough to justify their use. This Dia Compe Speedcheck system is particularly successful.*

disc and hydraulic brakes

Cantilever brakes which pull blocks onto either side of the wheel rim deliver outstanding performance in perfect conditions. However, when they are slightly worn, or if there is a little mud, water or dirt about their performance can drop off sharply. It's still good, but is well short of perfect.

That's where disc brakes come in. The hub-mounted disc brake is used on virtually all road vehicles as well as on aircraft, since it is clearly established as the most effective and reliable means of braking a wheeled vehicle. Using scaled-down motorcycle technology, it has also become the most effective means of stopping a mountain bike. The calipers press so hard onto the disc that less than perfect conditions have much less effect on the performance of these brakes than on wheel-rim cantilevers.

advanced technology

stopping power

The disc brake is not only superior in stopping power: with fewer working parts the hydraulic versions are probably easier to maintain than a cantilever brake, which can be fiddly. The hydraulic versions are also particularly suitable for full-suspension bikes with strange rear-frame designs, where it can be a problem to route a cable, which relies on minimum friction to work well, and also to mount the calipers when there are no seat stays. However, although there are plenty of different purpose-designed disc brakes for mountain bikers to choose from, they remain fairly restricted in use for two good reasons:
1. Disc brakes are expensive, most models costing considerably more than the most expensive cantilever brake.
2. Disc brakes are heavy. On average, a typical disc brake adds 7oz. This is the real sticking point.

If manufacturers can get disc brakes down to a competitive weight and also reduce their price, we shall certainly see a lot more of them. Purpose-designed suspension forks with mounts for specific disc brakes will almost certainly be necessary, together with new wheels to accommodate the discs.

● below left Suspension bikes don't have to follow the same outline as rigid bikes, and this Muddy Fox Interactive bike seems to try harder than most to break the mold. This design links the front and rear wheels so that hitting a bump with the front fork compresses the back at the same time.

● below right This is the man who really got the suspension revolution going. Paul Turner decided to scale down motocross forks and put them on a bicycle. Many years down the line his company, Rock Shox, still leads the field.

suspension trends
the need for suspension

Front-suspension forks for mountain bikes began to appear at the end of the 1980s, based on motorcycle and moto-cross technology and led by the American manufacturer Rock Shox. The initial disadvantages were weight, reliability, and cost, plus a general disbelief in the benefits of using them. However downhill racers soon found that suspension forks greatly improved their speed and control on rough terrain, putting them clear ahead of those riding rigid-fork bikes. Their superiority for cross-country use took longer to establish, but by the mid-1990s, as the choice of suspension forks got wider, few pro riders would be seen without them. The units had become much lighter, more reliable and more predictable in their performance, though their cost remained high.

Rear suspension followed close behind, opening up the prospect of "full-suspension" bikes. At first the concept was held back by factors similar to those that had delayed the adoption of front-suspension forks – cost,

weight, and considerably greater complexity as the designs of bike frames began to undergo some radical changes. When World Mountain Bike Champion Henrik Djernis agreed to race with the full-suspension ProFlex team in 1995, it seemed at last that the seal of absolute approval had been given and that all pure mountain bikes of the future would opt to follow the full-suspension route, while rigid forks and rigid tails were left behind.

front suspension

Front-suspension forks can be divided into those which use elastomers and those which use air/oil hydraulic systems for their shock absorbers. Coil springs, as used in motocross, are potentially more efficient, but are reckoned to be too heavy for front-suspension use. Most front-suspension units are based on a telescopic dual fork/shock design pioneered by Rock Shox. The exceptions are linkage forks, which combine rigid forks with a single shock absorber mounted beside the headset.

air/oil shock absorbers

In this system the suspension effect is provided by a mixture of oil and air sealed under high pressure in a cylinder at the base of each fork. As the front wheel hits the bumps the forks bounce up and down on the cushion of air. To prevent the bounce getting out of control, a "damping" effect is provided by the hydraulic oil. As the fork goes down on each compression stroke, the oil squirts into the air chamber through a tiny hole. As the fork goes up on each rebound stroke, the oil is sucked back. The damping effect can be regulated by controlling the flow of oil. On most suspension units this is done by turning a simple hand-operated plus-and-minus control knob.

● left *For competitive downhilling, full suspension is essential. At the highest level, it's clear that a good suspension bike can gain you the hundredths of a second you need to win. Active suspension that works all the time is worth a good few seconds on a tough course.*

● left *Made by a giant in moto-cross, Marzocchi XC51s were a common sight on Kona and Diamond Back bikes in the early '90s. Marzocchi excel at quality production techniques and unique looks.*

advanced technology

Some early air/oil suspension forks were unreliable owing to leaking seals. This problem seems to have been overcome, and you can expect long life from a good quality air/oil suspension unit.

elastomer shock absorbers

Downhill racing is an extreme application for any type of suspension. For the less-testing cross-country riding, the elastomer front-suspension system is the choice for most riders. Elastomer suspension is controlled by a stack of small doughnut-shaped rings made of hard but compressible foam. These "elastomers", as they are called, are available in different densities, so they can be mixed and matched to suit individual requirements. The physical properties of the foam provide the necessary damping movement to control the compression and rebound of the forks up to a maximum travel of about 2in.

The elastomer suspension can also be adjusted by using the "pre-load" dial (usually sited at the top of each fork) to compress the elastomer stack to a greater or lesser degree. This adjustment slightly alters the effective length of the forks. The adjustable setting can also be used to provide a suspension to suit the weights of different riders, and also to speed up or slow down the suspension travel according to the terrain.

In general, elastomer forks are lighter and cheaper than air/oil hydraulic forks, and there is very little to go wrong with them. Maintenance on a high-quality set of forks should entail nothing more than greasing the telescopic sliders (as with the air/oil system), and replacing the elastomers every year or so. The elasticity of the elastomers deteriorates over a period, and its physical properties may also change temporarily with the weather. The elastomer stack can become harder in very cold weather and softer in very warm weather, and this will affect its suspension

characteristics. Extreme changes in temperature can also affect the performance of air/oil hydraulic systems by temporarily changing the viscosity of the oil.

oil with elastomers

Elastomer forks are excellent at coping with small bumps and lumps for general cross-country use. They have less initial resistance to movement on the compression stroke, but are not so effective at controlling fork rebound over the longer distance. Nor can the damping be so precisely tuned to individual requirements. One answer may be to combine elastomers and hydraulics, as in Manitou Elastomer Fluid Control (EFC) and Rock Shox Judy forks. In this system conventional twin elastomer stacks are used to damp the compression movement, while a single hydraulic cartridge at the base of the left fork damps the rebound movement. There is a plus-and-minus adjustment dial for each elastomer stack and for the hydraulic system, giving extra scope for fine tuning.

● below *The Rock Shox Judy fork, introduced for the 1995 season, turned suspension upside down by combining the suppleness of elastomer forks, with the control of hydraulic forks.*

linkage forks

Linkage forks, such as the Girvin Vector, from the same team which originally developed the flexible suspension stem and built the Pro-Flex range of full-suspension bikes, is a system that uses rigid forks mounted beneath a single shock absorber which is aligned with the headset. Using an elastomer stack, this is potentially a simpler design than that of telescopic forks; it is light and rigid and very easy to maintain.

rear suspension

There is absolutely no doubt about it: if you are riding on tracks and trails with anything in the way of lumps and bumps, an efficient system of front and rear shock absorbers providing full suspension is best. Front suspension will help to take the load off your hands, but the rigid tail of your bike will jump around unless it, too, is able to cushion the bumps.

While front suspension can be fairly easily installed by changing the forks, the whole geometry of the bike is affected much more dramatically by rear suspension. Designers have a number of conflicting

● left *Designing the perfect rear suspension system is a tough job on a mountain bike, because of the limited drive-power that the rider puts out. Motorcycle systems can be designed to absorb some power, because there's always more at the flick of a wrist. Bike suspensions must be as efficient as possible.*

● above *Using a minute linkage, a short coil spring and one of the smallest dampers you're likely to see, AMP forks offer another option in the front-suspension battle. They work well over small and large bumps, and are some of the lightest units available.*

● **above** *Complex rear suspension designs mean that getting the brake blocks to hit the rim can be a problem. This San Andreas gets round the braking problem by using an in-house designed disc brake to do the stopping.*

● **right** *Suspension bikes are designed by putting the tubes where they need to be, rather than where they used to go. Elements of this Klein look like a regular bike, but put together as a whole it looks like it's from another planet.*

● **top right** *Typical of an early production suspension bike, this Diamond Back used small diameter steel tubing and a slim swingarm, resulting in a ride that wasn't stiff enough for many riders. They improved the bike after this.*

problems when dealing with rear suspension:
● If the distance between the bottom bracket and saddle changes owing to the action of the suspension, pedalling efficiency will be reduced.
● If the distance between the bottom bracket and the rear hub changes, the length of the chain will be affected and will reduce the efficiency of the drivetrain.
● The rear brake and derailleur cables must continue to operate efficiently, even though the rear of the bike may move independently of the handlebar area with the control levers. In some designs routing the rear brake cable can be a problem which can be solved only by using a hydraulic brake system.

Air/oil shock absorbers have been widely favored for rear suspension, but may soon be overtaken by the use of the coil spring for serious downhill use. For cross-country and recreational use, the simplicity and cost effectiveness of the elastomer system seems likely to prove most popular.

design ideas

By the mid-1990s designers were experimenting with a host of ideas to deal with the rear suspension problem, including the following:

● **The cantilever beam** The simplest system, this uses a single rigid beam, usually sprung on an air/oil shock absorber with one pivot point. It gives a long range of travel which makes it a favored system for downhill racers, but the arm needs to be extremely strong and so is likely to be too heavy (and look too primitive) for cross-country cycling enthusiasts.

● **Twin shocks** This simple system, favored by Marin, doubles up on elastomer suspension forks front and rear, using a conventional rear triangle with two pivot points at the top and bottom of the seat tube. Owing to the design the length of shock travel is limited, which makes it best at handling terrain with moderate rather than extreme bumps; so it is not suitable for top-class downhill racing.

● **The MacPherson strut** With its combination of light weight, simplicity, and good performance, this system has been widely used for full-suspension bikes. The basic outline of the rear triangle remains the same, with three pivot points; but the two seat stays are substantially beefed up to connect the shock absorber to the frame. Using a conventional frame shape, the strut is inclined to be overlong, which can lead to problems with flex. To overcome this, manufacturers such as ProFlex re-designed their main frames with radical-looking "interrupted" seat tubes which allow the use of a shorter strut.

● **Rising rate/Parallel linkage** This system, used by GT and Specialized, is a refinement of the MacPherson strut which puts in an extra pivot point, creating a four-sided rather than triangular rear frame. It allows the shock absorber to be mounted in a choice of positions, with dual pivot points at the top and bottom of the quadrilateral that supports the rear wheel. It can be used to enable the rear wheel to move up and down in a much tighter vertical movement than the arc of rival systems, and with minimal lateral flex. This is theoretically an extremely efficient way

of keeping the power wheel firmly on the ground, but it is possibly the most difficult rear-suspension system to design correctly.

● **Unified Rear Triangle (URT)** URTs, also known as "floating drivetrains," have been heralded as a breakthrough by big-name manufacturers such as Klein, Schwinn, and Trek. In this system the frame is effectively divided into two halves, with a single pivot point and with a shock absorber mounted vertically between the saddle and bottom bracket. The drive between the chainwheels and the rear sprockets is constant since, unlike that of most rival systems, URT suspension and drivetrain are separately mounted. The distance between the saddle and bottom bracket will vary, so careful engineering is required to make the single pivot sufficiently rigid.

One interesting feature is that the suspension is primarily activated by the weight of the rider. When he sits down on the saddle and is in greatest need of suspension to cushion the ride, the shock absorber will work to maximum effect. When he stands on the pedals the system will partly "lock-out" and cease to work so hard. The degree of lock-out can be adjusted, giving

● above left *Yeti spend a lot of time testing their products on the race track.*

● above right *Though it might look like their regular model, downhill riders are often trying out new tricks.*

● below *Is this the shape of things to come? The 1995 trade shows were full of companies showing 1996 bikes with a swing-link rising rate suspension system.*

the rider the option of transforming the bike into a rigid-tail machine simply by getting off the saddle.

why full suspension is best

The principal disadvantages of full-suspension bikes are that they are more expensive, heavier, and more complex than rigid-tail bikes. Economies of scale will help bring prices down as full suspension comes to be regarded as the mountain-bike norm. The equipment will become lighter as it becomes more sophisticated, and full-suspension bikes should carry only a small weight penalty over rigid-tail bikes. So long as a system is carefully designed and constructed, full suspension should require little extra maintenance. The pivot points should have self-lubricating pivot bushings, while the shock absorber should require only an occasional clean and grease to keep it working properly. However, with hard, extended use, it does seem possible that the whole triangle of a full-suspension bike might lose its rigidity over a period of time.

Suspension bikes are not inherently any faster than rigid bikes, but they are certainly easier to ride fast. Having the bumps smoothed out on a fast downhill makes the ride a much more relaxed affair and gives you the confidence to ride fast, while on level ground a system that irons out the bumps allows you to ride faster for less effort. This is even true on a steep uphill, where a suspended rear wheel is able to glide over any lumps rather than stalling against them, allowing the rider to maintain a steadier pedalling rhythm than the off-on cadence needed to power a rigid-tail bike. Furthermore, if the pivot of the suspended rear triangle is high enough, it will also have the effect of pushing the rear tire down harder onto the ground for better traction, which is what a successful uphill is all about.

wheels and spokes

A bicycle wheel is composed of a rim that is suspended by wire spokes on the central hub. It is a sophisticated and highly stressed object, and there has to be a trade off between a light weight and strength. The lighter the wall thickness, the lighter the weight of the rim. This can be made more rigid by using a slight V section, but strength is the ultimately vital ingredient. The wheels of a mountain bike – and in particular the front wheel – have to absorb a great deal of shock without flexing or buckling, with the tire and the spokes cushioning and absorbing the impact of a bumpy ride. The walls of the rims have to endure a great deal of wear from the constant biting of the brake blocks, an action that will in time wear them away.

The wide rims usually found on mountain bikes are inherently strong, and in any case the very narrow rims on road-race bikes are not suitable for use with the wide tires necessary to cushion a rough ride. The norm for fast mountain-bike riding in reasonably easy off-road conditions is for rims to be 26in in diameter and 1–1.5in wide; if the ground is very rocky and a bike is making a fast descent, rims up to 2in wide will

left Wheels have to take an extraordinary amount of loading. They're stronger than you think, but they're not unbreakable. What makes them break is large sideways loading, which usually comes from bad landings or crashes.

far left Invented in the early 1900s, the quick release lever makes it possible to lock your wheels into your frame quickly, easily, and securely.

left Tires can radically affect how your bike performs, and it's important to get the right ones for the sort of riding you're doing. Fat, aggressive tyres are fine for rugged terrain, but for road use you need something thinner that will roll more easily on smooth terrain.

advanced technology

support bigger tires that help cushion the ride and cut down the risk of punctures caused by the inner tube being pinched on the rim.

The norm for mountain bikes is to have 32 spokes of 14/16 gauge stainless steel, each spoke having double-butted (extra-thick) ends to make them more rigid at the hub and rim while saving weight in the middle. Spoke tension is adjusted with a key at the rim, which ensures the wheel stays in alignment. Occasionally spokes may need tightening, as they stretch while a high-performance wheel wears in.

Carbon-fiber spokes are available at a high price, but have made little impact on the mountain-bike scene. Carbon aero wheels with a deep rim and from three to five solid carbon spokes have also been tried on mountain bikes. These are successfully used by road and track bikes to cut aerodynamic drag at high speeds, but they are heavier than conventional wheels.

tires for all uses

There is a huge choice in tyres to fit the standard 26in mountain-bike wheel. Their main features are:

● Widths, which range from 1–2.5in.
● Weights, which range from a little over 7oz to close to 35oz depending on width, construction, and the amount of tread. Lighter tires give much better acceleration at slow speeds, but heavier tires may provide more precise off-road handling at high speeds.
● Tread patterns, which range from a smooth pattern for road use to a deep, knobbly pattern to maintain grip in all off-road conditions.
● Construction, which varies depending on factors such as the number of threads per inch (TPI) in the casing, softer or harder rubber compounds for the tread, and the use of kevlar rather than steel beads.

● above *The spokes come from the hub to the rim, and when tensioned correctly they make the whole structure strong enough to take the load that you exert on them.*

● left *Pick a tire, any tire . . . but make sure it's the right sort. Consult a good shop for the right model for your particular sort of riding.*

● opposite top left *Specialized Ground Control was the first good offroad tire, and it's still one of the best. Made with a mid-sized casing and a tread that works as well in muddy conditions as it does in dry.*

● opposite top right *Trek's Big Kahuna tire is another good rough ground model. Generally, any mountain bike tire will fit on any mountain bike rim, and any brand of tire on any brand of rim. You don't have to stick to what came with the bike.*

road tires

The first category of mountain-bike tire is primarily for use on tarmac roads and the smoothest trails. Their main requirement is a low rolling resistance for a fast ride, and their typical features are a shallow tread pattern designed to give sufficient grip in wet weather or on loose surfaces, combined with a narrow width of 1–1.5in maximum. Typical tires giving maximum performance in this class are the very narrow, very light Specialised Turbo, and the slightly less extreme Ritchey Crossbite. All tires for road use should be pumped to the maximum recommended pressure.

off-road tires

Dedicated off-road tires have developed in sophistication to such a point that they can rotate effectively only in one direction. Some manufacturers recommend different tread patterns on the front and back tires, as on the Onza Rip and Rail brands. This is the world of extreme tread, generally from 1.5–2in wide but sometimes almost 2.5in. The wider the tire, the greater is the volume of air to cushion the impact of very rough riding, and the greater is the rolling resistance on smooth surfaces. The deeper and more pronounced the tread, the heavier the tire is likely to be; and weight also increases with width.

These tires are specially designed to deal with mud, wet grass, loose surfaces, dirt, or rocks. At the messy end of the scale, mud

● above *Punctures come in all shapes and sizes. Here, the tires popped off* *the rim causing the latex tube to balloon to enormous proportions.*

and wet grass demand a tire tread which gives a precise grip without collecting and retaining the mud, which soon adds weight and clogs up the frame and forks. This problem is best dealt with by a pronounced tread on a fairly narrow 1.5in tire such as the Specialized Storm Control. A more open, deep tread deals better with loose dirt, while for hard-packed ground a tread with lower rolling resistance is necessary and a soft rubber compound grips best. It also wears quickly, and top racers will think nothing of changing a set of tires at the end of a hard race. The same tires will last considerably longer for leisure use, but it is worth checking the estimated life expectancy when choosing a new set of tires.

tire construction

The cost of mountain bike tires has risen fairly rapidly as they have improved in sophistication, getting lighter and gripping more effectively. It's worth checking out where the money goes, as a tire is a surprisingly complex creation.

The base of a tire is the casing, which is made of thousands of fine cotton or synthetic threads. These are woven in a two-ply cross pattern, and the number of threads per inch (TPI) helps determine the weight, flexibility and ultimate price of the tire. Tire casings with a greater number of fine threads are generally more supple, and this quality helps to improve cornering and lower a tire's rolling resistance.

The exposed sidewalls of the casing are potentially vulnerable, and often have a protective rubber coating. The thicker the rubber the better will be the protection, but the heavier and less supple the tire will be. At the base of the sidewall the tire is held onto the wheel rim by fairly rigid steel beading made of wire or kevlar. Kevlar is lighter, but can make a tire twice as expensive. Where the sidewall is forced against the sharp edge of the rim, extra protection is provided by a chafing strip.

On the outer side of the tire the tread is made up of a rubber compound bonded to the casing. Shallower treads are more supple, but obviously tend to wear faster because there is less depth. Some tires feature a kevlar band under the tread to help resist punctures from thorns, but this increases rolling resistance by making the tire less supple.

mudguards and crud catchers

If you are out on a mountain bike in wet weather, there is little doubt that you will get splattered. The deep tread of a typical mountain-bike tyre is great for throwing up mud and dirt. The front wheel will lift it straight into your face, while the back wheel showers your back with mud as well as bombarding anyone following close behind. Apart from avoiding muddy and rainy conditions, the only answer is to use

● below *An essential for leisure riding in the wet, a Crud Catcher is perhaps the simplest, most effective way of stopping your face getting sprayed by your front wheel.*

mudguards – so why are mountain bikes so rarely fitted with them?

The number one reason has to be that they don't look good. The number two reason is that if there's a lot of mud about, conventional road-style mudguards will soon lead to clogging between the tire and the inside of the guard. The best answer may be a guard such as the Crud Catcher which fits on the down tube directly above and behind the front wheel. It catches at least some of the muck, without causing any clogging.

inner tubes

Virtually all mountain-bike wheels are fitted with butyl inner tubes. In the early days of mountain biking Schraeder valves were popular. These use the same-diameter fitting as those on car inner tubes, which makes them convenient and simple to use. Nowadays, however, the lighter, more sophisticated Presta valve is favoured for high performance since it allows the tire to be inflated to a higher pressure.

Tire manufacturers always recommend a maximum pressure rating, which should generally be adhered to for best performance. This is usually printed on the sidewall of the tire in pounds per square inch (PSI). If a tire is blown up hard it will have a reduced ground contact area, which should give a hard, fast ride. If the pressure is reduced it will give a softer more forgiving ride, and possibly grip better in loose or slippery off-road conditions. In either case performance is likely to alter when using a variable suspension system.

The obvious thing that goes wrong with inner tubes is punctures. The most common form is a pinch puncture, which is caused when the tube is forced hard onto the rim owing to a sudden impact, such as hitting a small rock during a high-speed descent. The second most common cause of punctures is a thorn piercing the tire. Such punctures are usually easily repaired. Every mountain biker should be familiar with changing or mending a tube out in the wild, and carry the tools to do it.

advanced technology

● left *Everyone should know how to fix a puncture, because it's one of the most common problems on a mountain bike. Thankfully, it's not too common, due to thicker tyres and chunkier treads.*

pumps

Always carry a pump. It's vital! Many pumps have an adaptor which allows them to be used with both Schraeder and Presta valves.

● A good pump for recreational mountain biking is a frame-fit pump such as the Mt Zefal ATB Double Shot. This will fit snugly along the seat tube of many standard frames between the top tube and bottom bracket without the need for any special mounts. "Double shot" (or "double action") means that the pump puts air into the tube on both the up-stroke and the down-stroke, thus delivering air twice as fast.

● The conventional old-fashioned style of bicycle pump with a flexible connector tube may not look sleek, but it should not be despised. It is considerably cheaper than frame-fit pumps, as well as being potentially lighter. With a wide body, it can have a high single-action air output, but it will require clips or braze-ons to secure it to the frame.

● Some riders opt for mini or micro pumps which are considerably smaller and lighter than either the frame-fit or conventional pump. A model such as the Buddy Double Action Micro is just 7.5in long and weighs 3½oz. However, it is probably best not to get too carried away by the attractions of minimalism. If it comes to a puncture, a miniature pump is not likely to be able to put the air back into the tire as easily or as fast as a bigger pump.

● The last, most radical and most expensive option is a mini carbon dioxide (CO_2) inflator such as the Air Zefal. This will inflate a tire in a few seconds by a precise amount. It's far lighter, more compact, and faster to use than any pump, but it is used only once and then discarded.

● A track pump for home use is a luxury which many mountain bikers consider a necessity. With a big barrel, double handle, and foot-stand, the track pump puts in the air with maximum efficiency, and should be fitted with a gauge.

A Standard track pump;
B The Buddy Double Action Micro Pump;
C Mt Zefal Mini Double Shot;
D The Superflate, mini carbon dioxide inflator.

advanced technology

fixing a flat

Mending a puncture is a vital skill which should be learned as soon as possible. By the very nature of mountain biking punctures can happen quite frequently, though luck and careful riding can have a lot to do with avoiding them. Get to know the routine straightaway.

As soon as you feel a tire go flat, stop riding. If you ride on, you risk crashing, as well as possibly ruining not only your inner tube but also the tire and wheel rim. The repair is going to take a few minutes, so carry your bike to a comfortable and level location:

❶ Turn the bike upside down. At this stage work out where you're going to put things down: it's easy to lose the little valve cap in the undergrowth, and black plastic tire levers can disappear as well.

❷ Undo the brake straddle wire to open up the cantilevers, flip off the quick-release lever at the hub, unscrew the skewer if necessary, and remove the wheel. This is a more complicated job with the back wheel, owing to the sprockets and derailleur.

❸ You won't get the tube out unless it is well deflated. Carefully insert a lever to get the tire wall off the rim without damaging the inner tube, and then work the tire off all the way around one side of the wheel. Depending on the tightness of the bead, you may be able to do this operation without levers – or may need to use two or even three of them.

❹ Pull the tube out of the tire. If you're carrying a spare tube, move straight on to stage 6/7. If not, you have to find where the tube is punctured. If this is not obvious, inflate the tube, and then slowly pass it close to your ear and cheek. You should hear or feel the leak and be able to locate it. If this fails, you can try submerging the tube in a puddle and watch for tell-tale bubbles.

5 Keep a finger on the puncture. Roughen the surrounding area with the "roughener" provided in your repair kit, and then cover the area with a patch-sized blob of glue and allow the glue to set. (Some tire-repair kits have self-adhesive patches which speed this up.)

6 Very important! You have to find out what caused the puncture. Run your fingers round the inside of the tyre, find the cause, and remove it carefully.

7 The glue should now be set enough to put on the patch, which will bond straight to the tube. Now inflate the tube just enough to give it a circular shape; this makes it easier to get the tube back on the rim and avoid pinching the tube between rim and tyre. Finally, get the tire back onto the rim, using the levers when it gets hard to work the bead over the edge.

8 Push the wheel hub into the drop-outs. Connect the brake-straddle wire and pull the brake full on to ensure the wheel is centred before you tighten the quick-release hub. (It will also ensure that you don't ride off with the brake undone!) Now fully inflate the tire.

pedal pushers

toeclip pedals

The simplest and least efficient type of pedal is a platform or cage mounted on a spindle. Fitting it with a toe-clip and toe-strap ensures that you place your foot in the correct position, with the ball pressing on the spindle; the clip and strap also allow you to lift the pedal on the up-stroke. Toe-clips are made of stainless steel or unbreakable plastic. The main requirement is that they be light, and spring back into shape if you accidentally tread down on them. The straps should be made of a thick nylon weave or leather, and should help to maintain the shape of the clip for easy access, with a quick-release buckle to tighten or loosen them.

using toe-clips

The foot action for getting into and out of toe-clips is fairly easy once you're used to it.

The tighter the straps the better your pedalling will be, but the more difficult it will be to slide a foot out when you want to stop. Tightness depends on your confidence and riding style. If you ride long distances without putting a foot down, and are likely to have enough time to reach down and loosen the strap when a stop is required, you can afford

● above left *Clips and straps provide a secure fit, though it's nothing compared with clipless pedals.*

● left *Halfway between toe-straps and no-toe straps, Powergrips are an option for secure pedalling but give you the option to get out of them . . . fast!*

advanced technology

to pull both straps tight. If you regularly put a foot down, or are not sure when you're going to need to do so next, leave the left strap loose enough to slide your foot out without difficulty.

clipless pedals

Toe-clips are something of a hassle and are now less and less used by serious riders. To make them efficient, road racers would pull the straps really tight and wear hard-soled cycling shoes fitted with cleats. The old cleats looked like wedges and locked onto the ridges of the pedal; they were the forerunners of the modern clipless pedals, which every self-respecting mountain biker now uses.

Using a clipless or "step-in" pedal which locks onto your shoe is like switching into overdrive. Nothing else can give such a precise pedalling motion, and being able to pull up on the pedal with such efficiency is a major bonus when you need to really twirl the

● right *Shimano's top-of-the-range 747 replaced the 737 off-road pedal.*

● below *Shimano's innovation with SPD changed the face of mountain biking. Clipless pedals made mountain bikes far more manoeuvrable, and made jumps and reliable landings a thing to be looked forward to.*

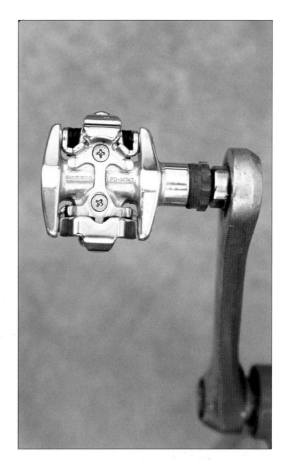

pedals on a difficult uphill. There are disadvantages, but overall they are not important. Clipless pedals are considerably more expensive than the old pedal and toe-clip, and they require a dedicated (compatible) pair of shoes. They are much heavier, have mechanical parts which need looking after, and are vulnerable to clogging with mud. They also require a slightly different technique. But once you've got the hang of them a good pair of clipless pedals are the only ones you will ever want to ride with.

Shimano was first on the clipless pedal scene for mountain bikers with their SPD system, which is still the benchmark by which rival products are judged. All clipless pedals work on principles similar to those pioneered and still used by Shimano. The pedals, which are made of aluminium and steel, can be used only with a dedicated shoe incorporating the correct cleat. They are fitted with a spring-loaded locking mechanism to hold the cleat, which is adjusted with an allen key for anything from a loose to a tight fit. The pedal is easier to use if it has locks on both sides of the pedal, though with a one-side lock the pedal will be lighter.

Rival clipless pedals to Shimano use steel, aluminium and sometimes titanium spindles and components, and have cleats which may not be compatible between different brands. Some, such as the 12½oz Onza Ho, are considerably lighter than the 18oz of the top-class Shimano PD-737. Onza manage this by using elastomers rather than spring locking, but the mechanism is less precise. Mud extraction is another target area. As the pioneer in the field, Shimano experienced plenty of problems with mud retention. In very muddy conditions both the pedals and cleats can clog up and become unusable, which in the early days could have the effect of permanently locking riders into their pedals. Newer models have been designed to shed mud and keep it from seizing the locking mechanism. How effective this is depends on how much you walk and fill your soles with mud, for there is always a point of no return when the intricate mechanism of a clipless pedal will not be able to cope without a wash-out.

Another rider problem with clipless pedals may be the degree of "float" – that is, the extent to which your foot can move sideways on the pedal. If the foot is held at a rigid angle, riders very occasionally experience knee problems. Other riders simply prefer freedom to twist their feet slightly on the pedals, feeling that this gives them better control when executing manoeuvres. Some clipless pedals allow more float than others, which can be adjusted by tightening or loosening the locking mechanism.

● below *SPD pedals must use special SPD shoes, with bolt holes in the bottom for the cleat to attach. The shoes are of rigid construction to give full power transfer and the best may use carbon soles.*

● below right *A steel cleat bolts to the base of the shoe, and then the jaws of the pedal grip onto it. With gaps for the mud to fall through, clipless pedals work well most of the time, but can become unusable in extremely dirty conditions. They can also freeze in the snow.*

using clipless pedals

1. Get used to locking in and out of the pedals before you set off. You'll need to lean the bike up against something, or have it supported, in order to practice the precise and fairly forceful foot action that is needed to lock in. Start with the tension loose, so that your foot comes out easily when you want it to but remains locked in when you back-pedal.

2. Clip in with your right foot, then push off. You should be able to clip in on the first down-stroke of the left pedal, though it doesn't matter if at first it takes a few more strokes. You may initially find it difficult getting your feet in the right position for the cleat to lock in without looking down, fiddling with your foot, and wobbling. But after a little practice this skill comes automatically every time.

3. With most clipless systems you clip out by twisting your heel sharply outwards; with others you have to lift your heel. Make sure this movement comes easily, so you are confident of clipping out instantly and can get a foot down on the ground within a second every time.

4. Once you are totally confident with your clipping in and out, tighten up the locks until you get a precise grip on the pedals which you are happy with at all times.

5. Keep your clipless pedals free of mud and dirt. Hose them out as required, and lubricate the whole unit regularly, using a light spray grease. The central spindle and bearings are likely to be housed in a sealed unit, and if so they will be almost impossible to lubricate without a major strip-down. But they should give long service without trouble.

cleat problems

One drawback of clipless pedals is that the cleats will eventually wear out and cease to lock properly, or the allen bolts holding them to the soles of your shoes may come adrift. The answer is to replace them whenever you give the bike a major overhaul. This may be difficult if the bolts are seized solid with corrosion, unless you had the foresight to use an anti-seize lubricant when installing them.

First give the cleat area a really good clean to remove all mud and dirt. If an allen key won't shift the bolts, try soaking the whole cleat area in penetrating oil for at least 24 hours. Then pour a kettle of boiling water over the cleat to make it expand. Hopefully you will now be able to undo the allen bolts.

If that fails you will have to drill them out, taking great care not to disturb the built-in nuts which are bedded in the shoe. Start with a 2mm drill, then move up to a 5mm drill until the head of the bolt comes away. You can then remove the old cleat, and attempt to unscrew the remaining threaded section of the bolt.

● below *One of the great advantages of clipless pedals is that there's no restricting strap holding your foot in place. This* *means that during those cold, wet times, there's less chance of your toes dropping off with cold.*

mountain-bike shoes

Mountain-bike shoes come in a vast variety of designs, most of which look pretty sporty. They range from all-out race-style shoes to more relaxed trainer-style sports shoes or hiking-style boots; most are designed for cleat compatibility. Which style you prefer will depend on how you ride, and in particular on how much you walk. If you seldom put a foot down and are pretty serious about riding, a dedicated race-style shoe will give the best performance. If you like to be able to hop off and push up or down steep hills, or maybe leave the bike and go exploring on foot, the sports or hiking-style shoe is the one to go for. The hiking style is probably more suitable if you habitually tackle really tough terrain.

With every kind of mountain-bike shoe the first requirement is that it should have a stiff, rigid sole. Road racers sometimes use solid kevlar soles for this purpose, but mountain bikers who may need to walk (or run if they're racing) on unridable terrain require a sole with a little more flex, particularly in the toe area. They also need a good grip on all surfaces including mud, and the soles of most mountain-bike shoes resemble the deep tread found on a serious off-road tire – some even include provision for non-slip studs for racing on grass. The earliest cleated road shoes had the cleats bulging out under the soles. This made walking almost impossible and mountain-bike shoe designers soon worked out how to

advanced technology

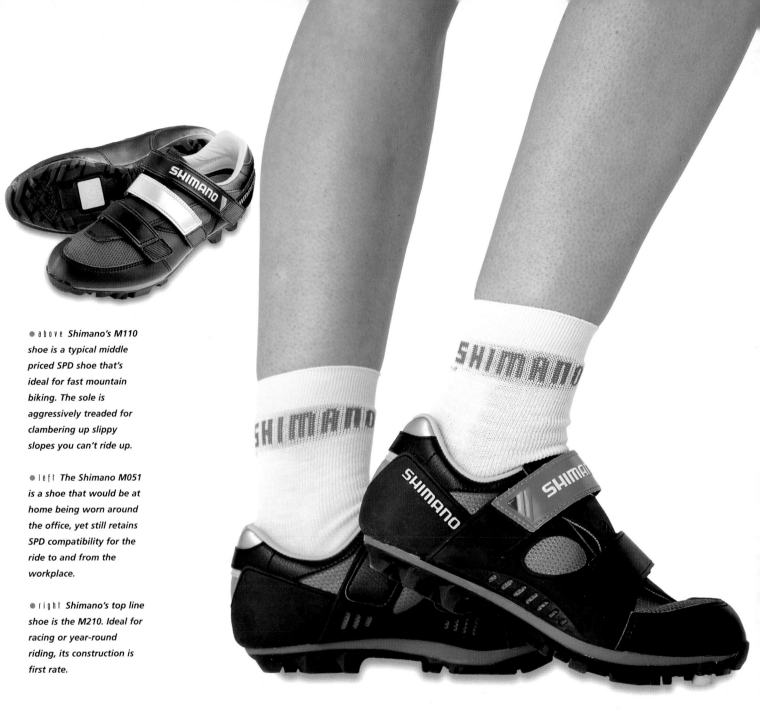

● above *Shimano's M110 shoe is a typical middle priced SPD shoe that's ideal for fast mountain biking. The sole is aggressively treaded for clambering up slippy slopes you can't ride up.*

● left *The Shimano M051 is a shoe that would be at home being worn around the office, yet still retains SPD compatibility for the ride to and from the workplace.*

● right *Shimano's top line shoe is the M210. Ideal for racing or year-round riding, its construction is first rate.*

recess the cleat into the sole, enabling the rider to walk normally.

The shoe should be a comfortable and precise fit. Laces still feature on some mountain-bike shoes, but many manufacturers have discarded them in favor of Velcro straps or more sophisticated fixings, such as the Sidi ratchet-buckle system. The uppers of most mountain-bike shoes are designed to be lightweight and cool on the feet. This is fine in hot, dry weather, but not so good if you ride in the cold and wet. Some

waterproof shoes and boots are available, but they are heavier than other types and may be uncomfortably hot in summer.

An alternative is to wear neoprene rubber overshoes in foul weather. These can be extremely effective at keeping the water out and the heat in, but are not suitable for walking. Keep your feet up on the pedals and they will give long service; but if you try to use them for rough walking they may soon fall apart as well as leak through the cleat holes.

4 mountain bike
specialization

XC racer

Self-sufficiency is at the heart of mountain biking. When you're out in the wilderness, and your bike breaks, you've got to ride it home somehow. Cross-country (or XC) mountain bike racing keeps the spirit of the rest of the sport in not allowing any outside technical assistance during the competition. This is at odds with the rest of cycling, where riders are allowed to swap tires, wheels, or complete bikes at their leisure. Food is allowed to be handed up during a race, but no tools, tires, or other spare parts may be handed up or assistance given.

● below *Until 1995 the most suspension racers would use would be a front suspension fork. In 1995 several racers, including the '94 World Champion Henrik Djernis, switched to full suspension bikes. Full suspension makes fast racing more comfortable.*

tracks

The courses that the races are run on are generally around 30–40 miles in length, with terrain varying from wide fire-road to narrow rocky singletrack. The bikes have to be capable of being hammered around these tracks for upwards of two-and-a-half hours, without breaking or fatiguing the riders unnecessarily. Weight is of course an important factor, and top riders have been known to quibble with their team mechanics about the addition of just a few grams. UK National Champion David Baker uses a minimalist titanium tool kit to further save weight aboard his ultra-lightweight bike every time he goes racing.

Historically, XC race bikes have been little more than an exercise in ultimate strength-to-weight compromises with many riders running laughably lightweight wheel combos, ultra-light bars and drilled out components to shed as many pounds as possible; still having a machine that would just carry them to the finish line. Indeed a famous frame builder has said that the ideal racing mountain bike would "Fall apart going over the finish line". The key to the bikes was that there was to be no more weight than was needed.

suspension

The advent of suspension in downhill racing coincided with XC racing going through a "rigid is better" phase. Everything was beefed up to maximum stiffness by using large diameter aluminium tubing to provide a chassis that concentrated on the power going into the wheels, and nothing else. Suspension forks were shunned at first, due to their "bobbing" when climbing, which the cross-country riders saw as robbing them of power. As it happens, movement at the front of a bike has absolutely nothing to do with the power going through the drivetrain; this is just wasted energy and dissipates no matter what the fork fitted is. It's possible to ride a suspension fork smoothly, and learning to do so makes you a more efficient rider; concentrating on turning precise circles, rather than throwing your weight around. The riders soon found that suspension forks, and lately full-suspension bikes, allow you to ride harder and faster without feeling as tired. In a race that's anything up to four hours long, any preserved energy is a good thing, and suspension allows riders to finish a race feeling less tired during the closing stages of a race.

The rest of the components on an XC race bike are chosen to suit the speed and terrain of the event. Gearing is often preselected, but a standard combination will

● left *A typical XC race bike will have an aggressive low stem, lightweight wheels and tires, a front suspension fork and be as light as possible. These guys quibble over grams!*

typically use larger gears than normal, to allow the riders to make the most of fast rolling downhills, or smooth fire-road sections. In the UK and Europe, there are few long, steep climbs on XC races; the short steep ones that do exist are normally taken by running, but some areas (notably the US) have long steep climbs in the areas surrounding ski-resorts where races are run. Here specialist gearing may be used to allow the rider to climb a 30% gradient for the several miles that may be on the course.

The tires and tube are mounted onto hand-built wheel assemblies, a place where further weight savings occur. Often, instead of having the 32 spokes of a production mountain bike, racing bikes may have as few as 28 spokes in a wheel. The rims will also be some of the lightest possible. Wheel assemblies are checked and tensioned before and after every race to avoid a disaster. A broken wheel is a no-ride option in most cases.

Handlebar, stem and saddle are all set to give a position close to that of a road bike,

● right *Ritchey bikes are always minimalist and clean. Using steel tubing, specially designed for each frame, Tom Ritchey constructs the chassis to be race strong, and nothing else. These frames are often retired after only a few races.*

tires

Tires are usually narrow, and pumped to a high pressure. Narrow, hard tires roll faster on hard terrain than their larger, softer brethren found on "normal" mountain bikes, and have the added attraction that they're lighter too. The high pressure is also used to guard against punctures which can easily cost a race. Some riders use heavy gauge inner tubes (those used for downhill racing) to further guard against pinch-punctures.

with the bars anything up to six inches below the saddle. Road bikes are where XC riders spend most of their time, as the pace of a race is so fast, and road-training is the only way to gain the fitness required for success at a high level. Bars are usually narrow, to give a position which gives comfortable breathing characteristics and allows you to steer through narrow gaps at high speed. It should be said here and now that many of the modifications that racers

● right *Racing isn't just about hammering on hard tracks. Sometimes the going gets rough, and riders have to battle against the elements as well as each other.*

employ aren't to the liking of the vast majority of riders. Bars well below the saddle and super-hard narrow tires don't give a comfy ride; but it is the optimum position for extracting the maximum amount of energy on smooth, hard terrain.

the essentials

To sum up then, these are the essential parts of a Cross-Country Race bike:
● Narrow tires pumped to a high pressure.
● Front suspension forks.
● Hand-picked gearing.
● Lightweight wheels.
● Bar, stem, and saddle set up like a road bike.
● Minimal lightweight tool kit.

● left *With riders training most of the time on road bikes, bar ends are popular on XC race bikes, giving a position like climbing on the brake levers of a road bike.*

downhill

downhill racing is now a sport that's so competitive that there are riders who do nothing else, bikes designed to do nothing else, and events where there's nothing else but downhill to watch. Its high speed spills and thrills have won the attention of the TV companies, bringing vast sums of sponsorship money into the sport. The riders competing in downhill races are usually paid more than their cross-country racing equivalents, which is reasonable when you consider the risks they take during the races. Downhill bikes are a showcase for full suspension. Though rigid bikes were once the norm in downhilling, once suspension became available the downhill racers were the first to embrace the new technology. Now many suspension systems debut on the DH circuit, before trickling down to the XC race level and finally into the market place.

● opposite *Myles Rockwell at a Grundig World Cup event, looking more like a motocross bike than a mountain bike. It's no surprise as these riders reach motocross speeds pedalling down super-steep hills, whatever the surface. 50mph is not uncommon.*

● below *Downhill bikes have to be built to do the job. Weight isn't really an issue, but strength is definitely important. Full suspension is the only thing that does the job properly. A rigid bike just won't cut it at the top level.*

When you're flying down a rough mountainside track, reaching speeds approaching 60mph, it pays to have a bike you can trust. Modifications from the norm when downhill racing is on the agenda include active, long travel full suspension, a riding position with more weight on the rear wheel, and super-wide, high handlebars to give positive steering characteristics.

suspension

There are no longer any riders on the World Cup downhill circuit riding anything other than full-suspension bikes. When speed is the aim, the better the suspension system, the faster the rider can go, and without full suspension you're giving yourself a handicap to start with. Just as in the rest of the sport, downhillers originally tried bikes which locked-out when they pedalled, but they now all want (even if they can't have) bikes that allow the suspension to move when pedalling or braking.

A typical downhill racing mountain bike, such as the GT LTS DH, is a bike that has been refined through input from World Champions Mike King and Nico Voiliouz. The bike features 5.5in of rear wheel travel, 3in of front wheel travel, all mounted on a chassis that weights the rear wheel, to allow the rider to stay seated through bumpy terrain, with the active suspension allowing him (or her) to pedal through the bumps. Front suspension is taken care of by the now almost obligatory Rock Shox Judy forks, giving 3in of travel.

tires

Tires are big, fat, and pumped to a pressure that's suitable for the course that's being raced on. Downhill riders are notoriously fussy about tyre selection. Some courses may require a tire that grips well in corners, while other courses may benefit from having a tire that allows the bike to drift when required. Tires are always at least 2.0in, mounted on heavy wheels that can take a beating.

gears

Gearing is chosen to allow pedalling on all sections. In downhill racing, if you're not braking, you should be pedalling. Speed is everything, with races being won by hundredths of a second, and so you've got to get as much speed out of the bike as possible. A downhill racer will use a conventional rear cassette cluster, and mix-and-match front chainrings to give a gear that's big enough to turn over on the fastest section of the course, but low enough to allow them to power out of the slowest corner. Normally a single large front chainring is used, along with some form of chain-guide to stop the chain jumping off the chainring. Ring sizes vary from course to course, but a downhill racer would keep sizes from 46–60 teeth in his tool kit.

handlebars

Upswept handlebars which are typical of those used by most DH racers nowadays. Their use has crept in over the last few years, with riders wanting a higher, wider position than that used by cross-country racers. The bars are usually the same as those used on motocross bikes, cut down slightly for a narrower position. They're mounted with the usual brake and shift levers, and often fixed into a "front loading" stem, that can be changed without having to remove all the components from the bike. This design allows the stem to be swapped for a model with a different reach or rise, to tune the bike's handling depending on the course. Very steep courses require a short position; longer stems are used on flatter courses where aero-positioning comes into play.

brakes

Braking is a mixed bag on most downhill bikes. Disc brakes are certainly the most

● above *John Tomac is dressed in an aerodynamic skinsuit for maximum* *speed on a downhill course.*

efficient stoppers out there, and there are an increasing number of riders using them, particularly on the front of the bike. Other riders use hydraulic brakes acting on the rim, such as those by Magura. These work well with the twists and turns that are needed to get the cables along the typical full-suspension frame, and work regardless of the position of the rear swing-arm. They are also incredibly powerful. Shimano has spent some time looking at the problem of braking on full suspension bikes, and for 1996 launched their V brake, a design which does away with the need for fixed cable-stops, and works well on full-suspension bikes. It is also far more powerful than a regular cantilever.

● below *A Proflex 954 full suspension bike. The elastomer suspension is* *much lower maintenance than oil and air.*

● above *Karim Amour in the Cap D'Ail, France, Grundig Downhill World* *Cup. The upswept handle-bars are typical of downhill racers.*

air management

Aerodynamics are starting to become an issue with speeds easily exceeding 60mph on some courses. It's a fair bet that they'll become more popular as other issues like suspension, braking and gearing become "designed out." If the rider wants to go faster, the aero has to be the way to go. Top downhiller John Tomac has been working with Mike Burrows, the designer behind Chris Boardman's Olympic Medal-winning Lotus track bike. The result is a fully faired downhill bike, but its one public outing so far only resulted in its being ridden around the starting area. It was too windy to use on the course proper. Yeti have experimented with minimal aerodynamics, and it seems certain that there will be some form of retrofittable aero components for suspension forks, seat posts, and maybe rims soon.

the essentials

To sum up then, these are the essential parts of a Downhill Race bike:

- Full suspension frame and forks
- Fat, heavily treaded tyres
- Hand-picked gearing
- Super-strong wheels
- Wide upswept bars and a low saddle
- Powerful brakes
- Aerodynamic details

mountain bike specialization

● right *One of the first true female stars of downhill mountain biking is Missy Giove. Racing as fast as some of the top men, she's a rider that many would like to beat.*

mountain bike specialization

● above *Trek 1995 full suspension bike, with carbon fiber frame and aluminum swinging arm.*

● right *Foes suspension bike, with aluminum frame.*

● above *Philippe Perakis's bike, Speed Week 1995 equipped with studded ice tires and front and rear disc brakes.*

● left *Christian Taileffer's bike, Speed Week 1995, also with studded ice tires and disc brakes.*

trials

a growing area of mountain biking is Trials. Developing from Cyclo-trials, a spin-off from motorcycle trials, it now exists in its own right, with the top riders earning good salaries by riding demonstration events at Shopping Center openings and Trade Shows.

Cyclo-trials use bikes with 20-in wheels, not unlike BMXs, but mountain-bike trials use machines with the industry standard 26-in wheel size; it's a little trickier to ride, but it means that anyone can compete on a "stock" mountain bike, rather than having to buy a small-wheeled machine.

● above *Trials are about doing things that people think aren't possible. None of this is of any real use in mountain bike riding, but boy, does it look good!*

● above right *Small-wheeled bikes are used for trials at the highest levels, though there's still a "stock" mountain bike class for bikes with 26in wheels.*

The bike frames look similar to normal mountain bikes, but are usually much shorter and lower. This is to give the riders more room to move. They're also usually much stronger than regular bikes, to let them withstand the forces that come from dropping off a large scaffolding tower onto one wheel.

One of the most important features of a trials bike is its brakes. They must be powerful enough that either wheel can be locked quickly and easily; usually with just one finger. For this reason, many riders use Magura hydraulic brakes, some even trying disc brakes. With the wheels locked, the bike can be hopped about, up steps, down steps, on either wheel . . . the list is endless.

To help the brakes grip the rim, many riders apply tar to the surface, which causes the brakes to stick to the rim far more keenly. The downside is that the brakes also squeak terribly.

Bars and stems on trials bikes are more like those from downhill bikes, than those on conventional production machines. The bar and stem set-up is what determines the weight distribution of the bike, and on a trials bike the weight must be divided between the front and rear wheels evenly, allowing either end of the bike to be picked up and flicked around. For this reason, a short stem and high rise bars are used; usually much shorter and higher than on other bikes.

Tires are the fattest around, and often run at very low pressures to enhance the grip. Tread patterns aren't usually that important as trials riders use their bikes on so many different surfaces; besides, tread designers don't spend a lot of time considering how to make tires to grip on wet car windscreens, or suchlike.

Because a trials bike is designed to be hopped around obstacles, some have just a single chainring and a standard rear cluster and rear mech. The gears used are very low; this gives good ground clearance at the front of the bike, and also means that it's easy to accelerate the bike in a short area, allowing easy wheelies; essential for trials manoeuvres.

● left and below *Hans Rey is one of the most dynamic riders in the world, and does a great job for his sponsors, GT. Hans is always trying more radical and dangerous tricks, looking around the world for trial problems to ride.*

the essentials

To sum up then, these are the essential parts of a trials bike:

- Strong frame and fork
- Fat, heavily treaded tires
- Low (often single-speed) gearing
- Super-strong wheels
- Wide, high bars and a low saddle
- Powerful brakes

expedition

Many people enjoy getting away from the hustle and bustle of society on their mountain bike, but for some people, a few hours isn't enough. There are lots of riders out there who get away from it all on their mountain bike for days or even weeks at a time. Mountain bikes are ideal for carrying large amounts of camping gear, either on roads or on trails. Really rugged terrain is possible, but obviously there's a limit to where you can go and enjoy yourself when you're hulking around too much gear.

● **below** *Expedition riding means carrying luggage, whatever the weather. Here front and rear panniers are used to carry the gear; enough for two days away from the world.*

● **below right** *Some types of riding demand special equipment. These riders in Alaska use handwarmers to keep them from freezing in the icy wasteland.*

A typical expedition mountain bike will have a frame made of high quality chromoly steel. This is one of the few areas of mountain biking where it's best to have a specific material. In all the other disciplines, all the materials have an equal footing, but in expedition riding, steel is the best material. Why? It can be mended the world over. Whatever town, village or settlement you happen to be in, there's a far better chance that your bike can be mended if it's made from steel, rather than from some of the fancy aerospace derivatives such as carbon fibre or titanium.

Wheels should be built to take a bashing. It's quite possible to carry up to eighty pounds of gear on a bike, over-stressing a standard set of wheels. Good

expedition wheels should have strong straight gauge spokes, brass nipples, and tough rims. Tires should be chosen depending on the surface that the bike has to go over. It may be a good idea to take spare tires with a different tread, if the bike has to cross rocky, then smooth terrain.

If you're wanting to carry a lot of gear, then it's best to carry it on your bike, rather than on your back. Racks are available to carry your equipment in panniers which mount securely, without bouncing loose on the bumps. They're available for the front or rear of the bike, with the best mounting securely to the frame by means of welded-on bosses.

For riding in the wilderness, a map case that fits onto the handlebars is a good addition to the bike, as it stops you having to unpack a map at every occasion. There are few good ones available on the market, so enthusiasts usually end up making their own.

For very cold weather trips, hand warmers are sometimes used. These are typical of the sort of additions that expedition riders make for special trips, well outside normal conditions. What the modification is will depend on where the bike is going. For extended desert trips, the ability to carry large quantities of water may well warrant a modification.

the essentials

To sum up then, these are the essential parts of an Expedition bike:
● Strong frame and fork made of steel tubing
● Tires to suit the terrain
● Racks and panniers
● Super-strong wheels
● Comfortable riding condition
● Specialist modifications

● above *Half the fun of battling against the elements is the feeling of satisfaction when you get back.*

● left *Want to ride in the desert? Though helmets are considered essential for most riding, you could cook your brain in one. In the desert use a large floppy hat, but take care on the downhills!*

trail bike

Your bike doesn't have to stay the way that it comes when you buy it. Local terrain affects the way that you ride your bike, and you can customize it to make the most of the conditions. I know people whose riding means that they have to ride under a lot of fallen trees. They all run low stems and small frames to help them scoot underneath. Other riders ride only on smooth twisting singletrack, and so ride bikes with rigid forks and hard tires. Other riders just go out and do big jumps, so they end up with a full-suspension bike.

What you need on your bike depends on the terrain you ride on, but here are some pointers for you, whatever the terrain.

If the position that you've got on your bike isn't comfy, then change it. Downhill bars are available that lift your position a couple of inches, and the stem can be changed for a higher rise model if you're uncomfortable with the position. Try putting your bars 1–2in below the saddle for a better riding posture. You'll be able to see where you're going much better.

Getting wheels built for you isn't cheap, but the strength and light weight they'll bring over cheaper production wheels is worth it. Over the years, the quality of wheels on production bikes has improved, but they're still nowhere near as good as a hand-built set. Invest in them early.

The right tires for your sort of terrain are important too. If you feel that your tires are letting you down, either by being too grippy or not grippy enough, then get a different set. Stop other local riders and ask them what they use, try their bikes. Tires can change the way a bike feels, and you can't get the best out of your riding if you're using sub-standard rubber.

Mudguards aren't the trendiest of things, but the Crud Catcher is a clip-on mudguard that works. Along with its sister component, the Crud Guard, they can ensure a muck-free ride for the most part. They're well worth having.

Tools are essential to a mountain biker. You can limit their use by making sure that your bike is always well adjusted, but they're needed because you never know what's going to work loose or bend when you're out on the trail. At the very least take along a pump, and a spare tube, as there really is nothing more depressing than pushing a bike home with a flat tire.

● left *A typical trail bike modified from stock. Features include a high stem, front and rear mudguard, quality suspension fork, and a comfortable saddle!*

the essentials

To sum up then, these are the essential parts of a Trail bike:

- Good wheels
- Terrain-suitable tires
- Comfortable riding position
- Toolkit, tube, and pump
- Mudguards

● left *Getting out in conditions like this means having to be with your bike all day. Customize it so it fits you and your style.*

● below *A high stem allows the bars to be in a position that is comfortable for the rider. Also, the higher position allows finer weight tuning between front and rear wheels, essential for tricky technical trails and aggressive riding.*

5 techniques-
advanced riding

what level do you ride at?

How easy or difficult it is to ride a mountain bike will depend on the terrain and how hard you push your own limits. A wide, smooth, dirt road will offer more rolling resistance than super-smooth macadam, but otherwise it should present no problem. At the other end of the scale a narrow, winding track strewn with tree roots and slippery boulders, and featuring steep climbs and descents, will tax your riding skills, fitness, and mental approach to their limits. Between those two extremes there are all sorts of levels of mountain biking to get out there and enjoy.

cadence and gear selection

The first thing to establish is cadence and gear selection. Cadence is the number of times the pedals are turned in a minute. The faster they go round the less leg-muscle force you will use to drive the bike forwards. If you pedal slowly in a high gear at the same speed you will use more energy, and if you keep changing the speed at which you pedal it will sap your strength still further.

The theoretical answer for peak performance is to maintain a steady cadence of around 80–90rpm. However on difficult off-road terrain this may be impossible, due

● above *Want to go fast? Really fast? Read on and get to grips with the techniques that you need to perform.*

to the nature of the terrain. One of the benefits of a full-suspension bike is that it allows you to pedal whatever the terrain is like.

Whether you are riding a rigid or full-suspension bike, do your best to keep the pedals spinning within the target range. To do this you must change gear as the terrain and circumstances alter, using the following simple formula:

● left *When descending hills, use the brakes as little as possible, and just keep up as steady a pace as possible.*

● below *Don't look up. Keep your mind on turning the pedals round, and try not to overwork yourself too early on.*

● When your legs are laboring it is time to change down through the gears.

● When your legs are racing, it is time to change up through the gears.

However, even that is not strictly true, since you should always change down ahead of time, choosing your new gear just before you get to different terrain. If you hit a steep section without changing down before you start to go uphill, you will usually find it impossible to drop a gear without easing off the pedals and losing momentum.

using gears

Many mountain bikes have a theoretical maximum of 24 gears (8 x 3), but do not assume you can use every one. You should never ride with the chain set at an extreme angle on the outer chainwheel and inner rear cog or vice versa. Apart from causing rapid wear to the chain, cog, and chainwheel, this is simply an inefficient way to pedal.

The chain may occasionally fall off the outer chainwheel when you change up on the front derailleur. Just stop pedalling, ease the derailleur guide inwards, and then gently pedal the chain back onto the teeth. If the problem persists or the chain drops off the sprockets on the rear wheel, the derailleur mechanisms will need adjusting.

techniques – advanced riding

● right *Braking is done by squeezing the levers, not grabbing them hard. Keep checking the trail ahead so that you know what's coming up, and try to avoid sudden braking as the bike can skid and you may well crash.*

● below *When descending keep looking where you're going. Don't look at the front wheel, or what it's about to roll over. Keep looking down the hill, picking the line where you're going to go next.*

using the brakes

Cantilever brakes in good working condition are powerful; disc brakes and those with hydraulics are even more powerful. The front and rear brakes should in most circumstances be used together, and should always be feathered to give a steady, even pull without locking either wheel. If you lock the rear wheel, you will skid, which does not help the environment; if you lock the front wheel you may well crash. How hard you pull on each brake is a matter of experience. For normal terrain a 70/30 rear/front action is likely to be about right.

Aim to use the brakes as little as possible, since it robs you of all the effort you have put into creating speed. When you have to brake, always think ahead, whether braking for a corner or on a steep downhill. A small two finger pull should be all that is necessary to brake effectively.

climbing hills

One of the main ingredients for success in climbing off-road hills is mind over matter. Just keep saying, "Yes, I can do it!" and you will get there. Mountain bikes have an extremely accommodating gear range which will tackle most slopes as long as the terrain, your technique and your physical fitness are up to it.

If the terrain is slippery – mud, grass or loose shingle – the main problem is likely to be maintaining rear-wheel traction. The rear tire should grip on most surfaces as long as it has enough weight to press it down. At the other end the front wheel may start lifting owing to the steepness of the climb, so you have to adopt a posture which puts the center of gravity firmly between the two wheels, adjusting your position to control rear-wheel traction and front-wheel lift as the slope and surface change.

All good quality mountain bikes are designed to allow the rider to maintain traction and control on the uphills, whether sitting in the saddle or standing on the pedals. Sitting down and twirling the pedals at a fast rate, while changing down through the gears as necessary, is the most effective way to climb long, steady hills. As the hill gets steeper, slide your weight forward until you are perched on the nose of the saddle. This is not as uncomfortable as it may sound, and some saddles are designed to be more accommodating in this area.

Standing up and stomping hard on the pedals while you push a higher gear at a lower cadence is the fast approach to a short, steep slope or a difficult uphill section with obstructions such as channels and gulleys.

● right *Correct gear choice means that climbing hills is made easier. By keeping a smooth cadence, a rider can maintain traction and momentum, climbing past the opposition. Bumpy surfaces need a lower pedalling speed, smoother surfaces need a faster one.*

The stand-up approach can be maintained only for a short distance, and if you blow up it becomes like the hare and the tortoise – the rider who sits down and twirls his pedals gets there first in the end. Standing up also makes it more difficult to control rear wheel traction. If the tire starts to lose its grip you should ease up on the pedals for a moment, readjust your body position, and then slightly reduce the power on the pedals.

● below *Standing up is fine on a fairly good terrain – otherwise, bad conditions can cause rear wheel imbalance.*

techniques – advanced riding

picking your line

It is also vital to look where you are going and choose your line carefully. Always pick the line of least resistance up the hill, and go for the grippiest surface. Look well ahead to search out the gentlest gradients, avoiding sudden rises that will sap your energy. Approach the climb at speed to gain enough momentum before changing into the correct gear for the main part of the climb. When climbing in the saddle on a steady hill, select your gear early and stick to it. If you need to change gear, choose your gears on the rear sprockets and stick with the middle chainwheel, avoiding dropping onto the smallest "granny gear" chainwheel for as long as possible. It is often better to stand up and drive the bike when it gets impossible to pedal sitting down. Once you are down in the granny gear it becomes that much more difficult to change back up to the middle

chainwheel if the slope gets easier, or if you suddenly need more speed to get past an obstruction. With practice this approach will build up your leg muscles for better climbing, and avoid the situation where you find you have run out of low gears.

With precise control on the center of gravity, it is also possible to lift the front wheel over obstacles such as rocks. Move back to take weight off the front wheel so that it lifts and then drops onto or over the obstacle. Power up to the obstacle with the back wheel, throwing your weight forward at the critical moment so that it follows you up and over without stalling.

● above *Try to go for the grippiest surface when picking your line – not always easy.*

● left *In competition riding, taking the right line is crucial – keep looking forward as far as possible.*

descending hills

Downhill off-road is all about having fun. Speed and enjoyment are directly proportional to the steepness of the hill, the riding surface, the width of the track, obstructions along the way, your technique and control, and your nerve when it comes to letting the bike run flat-out.

The fastest downhills are on easy, forgiving tracks with a good surface and not too much of a slope. There will soon come a point when your feet spinning the pedals will be unable to keep pace with the speed of the wheels, unless you have an oversize chainwheel specifically for downhill use.

The way to achieve maximum speed is to tuck your body into a crouched position

● right *Riding downhill can be hard enough but it's impossible without a front tire! If you're racing, you've got a flat, and the finish isn't far away, ripping your tire off is the fastest option.*

● below *Muddy conditions can be treacherous on a fast downhill, with the added disadvantage of impaired vision.*

like the "egg" shape adopted by downhill skiers. The cranks should be held horizontal, or lifted on the inside for bends; your knees should be pressed close together on either side of the top tube (on a conventional frame), and your backside lifted a short way off the saddle. Arms and legs should be braced and slightly bent to absorb the impact of bumps – front- and full-suspension bikes really come into their own when a downhill track becomes bumpy – with two fingers covering each brake lever in case you need to slow down. From there on it is just a matter of choosing the quickest, safest line down the hill which gives your tyres the best grip and least rolling resistance, as well as allowing maximum bike control, which is likely to be at its best with suspension. However, even with suspension you should take the smoothest route: the wheels will take a hammering even if it does not feel so bad on your body.

● left *Water riding is fun. When you hit the water, keep your weight back as your bike will slow down and may try to throw you off the front.*

extreme downhills

With good technique a mountain biker can drop-off on a near vertical descent. If the slope looks too steep, try some shallower slopes to build your confidence. You must start with a totally positive mental attitude that will allow you to hit the drop-off at the top of the hill knowing you are going to enjoy the ride to the bottom. If you panic, you will lose control.

To set your bike up for a radically steep hill it may be necessary to lower the saddle by as much as four inches. This means you can get your weight right back over the rear wheel and away from the front of the bike, with your stomach laid flat on top of the saddle. Raising the stem to lift the handlebars will help to move your center of gravity even further back.

The main object is to avoid allowing your body to go forward over the handlebars. The steeper the slope the farther back you will need to shift your weight, with your upper body at full stretch, two fingers covering each brake handle, and arms and legs slightly bent to absorb bumps. However, you still need to retain a position that puts the center of gravity firmly between the two

● left *Adjust your body position to match changes in the slope when going down steep hills, and keep checking your line.*

● right *Go easy on the brakes on very fast downhill courses. Let the bike run as much as possible and promote steerage by moving your body position.*

● right *If things go wrong, and you really have to go over the handlebars, tuck in your head and keep your elbows bent!*

wheels. If you move the center of gravity too far backward, you will lose control of the front end and be unable to direct the bike. Your body position must be constantly adjusted to match changes in the slope. Many riders make the mistake of shifting their weight back before they reach the steep drop-off. This means that control is lost at the start of the descent, and will be difficult to regain. The correct sequence is to adjust your speed and your line of approach in the final moments before the drop-off, and move your weight back only as the front wheel goes down.

Speed must be kept under control all the way to the bottom, allowing the bike to keep moving fast enough to stay balanced. You can always accelerate to gain speed if you are in control. Carefully feather the brakes, using an approximate 60/40 front/rear brake force, which will allow the rear wheel to follow down the hill behind you. Never jam the brakes on hard in a panic. Try to let the bike run as much as possible and promote steerage by moving your body from side to side. Always remember that when the tires are under a braking load they will cease to grip as well as when they are unrestrained. As long as the bike is moving forward you are unlikely to go over the handlebars. If the back wheel locks it will begin to skid and slide round. To cure this, release the brake lever momentarily, then ease it on again. If you lock the front wheel the consequences are likely to be more dire.

Keep checking your line all the way down, and look ahead so that you have time to react to obstacles and gauge the amount of run-out at the bottom. If things look bad, sliding off the back of the bike and landing on your backside is a much better idea than going over the handlebars. If you do get it wrong and go over the bars, you should tuck in your head and roll with your elbows bent.

airborne downhills

If you have the technique and are traveling fast enough, it is possible to hit the top of a hill at speed, take off, land further down the slope, and keep on riding. Before attempting this you must carefully check out the take-off, landing and run-out areas. If there are any obstructions, don't try it – you need a smooth slope, with a forgiving run-out at the bottom.

When you hit the lip at the top of the slope with enough speed your bike will automatically become airborne as the slope drops away. Lifting on the pedals should be avoided since it tends to tip you forward; lifting on the handlebars and leaning back will get you flying with the rear wheel in a safe position closer to the ground. Once airborne your weight should be centered over the bike, with your body relaxed and ready to absorb the impact of landing. If the bike starts falling to one side, try to drop the opposite shoulder. If the front wheel turns, ease off pressure with the stronger arm, which is instinctively pulling it round.

It is best to touch down on both wheels or, failing that, to land on the rear wheel first. Do not tense up in the air, as this will make the landing hard; do not touch the brakes as the wheels must be free to turn as soon as you land; do not lean forward and land on your front wheel, or you are likely to crash. Lowering your seat well down before take-off lets you move around more as well as lowering your center of gravity. The fatter the tires the better they will grip on landing,

● left *Time in the air is time wasted. But it's great fun to skim down a hill rather than pedalling.*

● above *Jumping down rocky, technical sections like this means that you don't have to worry about which line to take.*

● right *Over the top. This is what it's all about.*

though make sure they are blown up hard enough to absorb the impact without getting pushed onto the rim walls.

Jumping may look spectacular, but while you are up in the air there is nothing to pedal and the bike will slow down. For this reason mountain-bike racers tend to keep their jumps as short as possible. When they know their speed dictates that the bike must get airborne on the next ramp, they "pre-jump" the bike by doing a bunnyhop just before they hit the lip at the top of the slope. This means that, rather than being launched away from the slope, they execute a much smaller jump and land just on the far side of the lip, with minimum pedaling time wasted.

singletrack riding

The narrower an off-road track gets, the more difficult it can become. This is particularly true if there are obstructions such as roots, rocks, or trees or the track winds its way steeply downhill. "Singletrack" is a track which is basically wide enough for only one bike. Speed must be reduced and control carefully maintained because you will be unable to avoid hazards such as roots, rocks, and strange cambers.

The priorities for singletrack are to keep your bike and body in balance with the track. It is important not to get panicked by difficult surfaces into the sort of "I'll never make it!" mental response induced by a vertiginous downslope.

● below *Riding singletrack is a combination of fast weight shifts, keen reflexes and luck. You never know what's round the next corner, so sometimes you've just got to guess!*

The rider should try to keep his body centered over the bike to maintain balance and tire traction. For instance, total control can be maintained on a narrow bend by leaning the bike in and moving your hips out. Viewed from behind, an imaginary plumb line could be dropped from your head to the contact area of your tires, despite the acute angle that your body and the bike are making. While the bike is banked for the turn, your weight is directly over the area where the wheel tread hits the ground, so maximum traction is maintained. The same technique can be used for tackling tricky cambers where you come to a cross-slope, leaning your bike away from the slope while pushing your hips in to keep most of your weight over the wheels.

Always look well ahead, and size up what comes next. Aim for the smoothest line possible, and if you come to a particularly bad section, try to let the bike run with the brakes off and float over it. Roots and rocks which cannot be avoided can be negotiated by hopping the front wheel up and over, with the rear wheel following behind. If the bike stalls you can get off and walk, then go back and try again.

● above *John Tomac single track riding in the Grundig World Cup, Italy. Getting the lead in single track riding takes real expertise and stamina, especially when riding uphill.*

cornering

The optimum route through a bend is apex-gutter-apex or wide-tight-wide, though your line may have to be modified by natural obstacles such as tree roots, rocks, and difficult cambers. Choose your line carefully as you go into a bend at speed, looking ahead and maintaining enough control to change the line if required.

To slow down for a bend you should ease up on the pedals and do any braking that is necessary when the bike is travelling straight and before you start to turn. If you brake on the bend, you risk inducing a skid when the bike is at its least stable. This is particularly risky if the surface is wet and slippery. Lower your center of gravity by crouching as the bike goes round the bend, and lean into the turn if the speed requires it. To help the tires keep maximum traction on a tight bend, keep your body upright with your weight on the outside pedal.

On a sweeping bend you can usually pedal right through, avoiding using the brakes or changing gear if possible. On a tight bend where you will lose speed you will need to change down through the gears, selecting the right gear for a smooth exit as you pedal, coast or brake into the bend. Stop pedalling if there is any chance of your inside pedal hitting the ground on the bend, and hold it in the up position. As soon as the bike starts to come upright, pedal hard to accelerate out of the corner.

On a series of fast downhill bends, as on a forest dirt road zig-zagging down a hillside, lean well into each bend with the inside pedal in the up position and your inside knee pushed out at an angle. An alternative technique for fast riders is to drift through the bend with a controlled rear-wheel skid. This technique can be useful if a bend suddenly tightens up, or if you need to make a sudden change in direction to avoid an obstacle or another rider. It will leave your tyre marks on the track, so you need to be sure it is environmentally acceptable.

A skid can be induced on a loose surface or at high speed on a downhill bend by shifting your weight forwards before turning sharply into the apex of the bend, and if necessary jabbing the back brake to momentarily lock the wheel. As the rear wheel slides out, the rider turns the front wheel away from the bend to let the bike slide with the skid, using the opposite-lock technique used to handle a skid in a car. Careful steering with the handlebars will control the direction of the skid, but at very high downhill speeds it may be necessary to drop the inside foot to skim the ground for added stability before putting the power back on to exit the bend.

● this page and opposite *When you're cornering fast on loose terrain it pays to take precautions. Sticking a foot out means that you can drift the back wheel easily to bring the bike round onto the right line, and also catch yourself if the whole thing tips over.*

riding in mud

Riding in mud is like nothing else. It can require twice the pedaling effort for half the speed, it makes cornering slippery, and it clogs the moving components of your bike to the point where they can all stop working. In addition it makes you dirty. Your bike and your body will get splattered, and since mud is wet it will soon cool you down, particularly if it plasters your backside.

It is very important that your front and rear wheels have sufficient frame clearance to avoid clogging. Tires that perform well in mud should grip like leeches while throwing clear any dirt they pick up, which means

● above *When it gets to this point, you just have to stop and clean up the bike.*

● right *Mud riding is something you have to endure. Either take a fast approach and hope you skim through it, or plod through slowly maximizing traction as you go.*

techniques – advanced riding

having well-spaced, prominent tread knobbles. The mechanism that is most prone to clogging is the rear derailleur and sprockets. A device such as a Crud Claw mounted on the sprockets may help a little; otherwise all you can do is ride through puddles to clear the mud whenever possible, or stop and squirt the derailleur and sprockets with your water bottle.

The same problem may afflict clipless pedals, particularly if you are forced to walk the bike, which will also clog the cleats in the soles of your shoes to the point where they may refuse to lock onto the pedals. Again, a squirt from the water bottle is likely to be the best solution. If you also wish to drink some

water, the spout of the bottle must of course be protected from the mud to keep out bugs and filth and make it safe for drinking.

When you are faced with a short patch of liquid mud ("gloop"), it may be best to attempt to power through at full speed, keeping traction on both wheels. To get through long sections of gloop, you may need to change down so you can spin the pedals without sapping your energy before you reach the other side. Avoid getting stuck in muddy ruts, either those made by other bikes or deeper ruts cut by 4WD vehicles. If it is faster to get off and walk, you should do so; this will also help preserve the track from tire erosion.

● above *Whether it's the first puddle of the day, or just one of many, mud riding makes your bike filthy, but is, in some small way, a lot of fun!*

Cornering will require care if you want to get round without slithering. As you go into a corner the mud may slow you enough to obviate any need to pull on the brakes, but if you do need to brake, do so before the corner. At the same time change into the gear you will need to accelerate out, and set yourself up for as wide a line as possible through the bend (though that will depend on the conditions). If the bend is really slithery, be ready to drop your inside foot onto the ground and aim for the grippiest ground to ride on.

Riding uphill on mud, try to avoid braking or stalling. Keep to the smoothest, driest line up the hill to maintain traction, with your weight well back to hold the rear wheel down. Keep up a steady cadence, changing down to a lower gear as soon as you lose momentum or the tire starts to slip. If you need to stand up to drive the pedals harder, concentrate on maintaining traction on the rear wheel.

Riding downhill, choose your line carefully. Set your speed by braking before the drop, and then once you are on the way down try to avoid pulling on the brakes, which will almost certainly induce a skid. If you do need to brake, pull only very lightly with a 70/30 front/rear pressure to avoid locking up and sliding. Keep your body loose and relaxed, with a light grip on the handlebars and with the brake levers covered. Stay out of the saddle, letting the bike take its own route down. This means you should let the rear wheel remain fairly loose, with your legs and arms slightly flexed and your weight adjusted to keep the center of gravity between the wheels.

● left *Riding through the mud hole in competition at Vermont.*

riding through water

Big puddles which retain water usually indicate hard-packed ground which is safe and easy to ride through. However, sometimes the ground may be soft, or there may be underwater obstacles which will stop you in your tracks. There are two ways to ride through puddles. Number one is to select an easy gear before you hit the puddle, which will allow you to ride through slowly without soaking your body. This will also let you power out of trouble and onto dry land if the going gets difficult. Number two is to power through at high speed, which is intended to get you fast to the other side with a lot of spray on the way. In both cases, misreading the nature of the puddle can mean you will stall, fall off, and get very wet.

● below *Water riding is easy; you just need to keep going. Hit water fast with your weight forwards and you'll end up over the bars. Take it too slow, and you'll get bogged down.*

difficult surfaces

● Sand should be avoided if at all possible.
Fine sand is pernicious; it is almost impossible
to ride over without sinking, and it will leap
into a well-lubricated chain and grind its way
through your chaindrive and gear
mechanisms, making nasty noises as it
abrades the metal.

● Dry grass usually gives good traction, but
wet grass can be very slithery, especially if you
are going up or down a steep hill. The answer
is to stay relaxed and aim to ride on the
grippiest sections; but try to do this without
skidding and ripping open the turf with
your tyres.

● Surfaces such as wet shale, damp planks on
an old bridge, or a carpet of slimy leaves can
be very slippery. You must brake and regulate
your speed before you hit these surfaces,
then ride across keeping your bike on line
with an easy pedalling action while sitting
down. If you hit the brakes the bike will
almost certainly slide and may drop onto the
ground. Ice is the most slippery surface of all.
If you hit ice the golden rule is to go with it,
pedal carefully, never touch the brakes and
look for a way off it.

● Big tree roots should be approached as
nearly as possible at right angles to your front
wheel. The more slippery they are, the more

● below *Long grass can
conceal clumps and
potholes, so go for the
clearest area.*

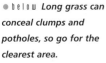

technique — advanced riding

important it is to hit them square-on. Lift up on the front wheel to guide it over the roots, then take some weight off the rear wheel to allow it to follow. Hitting roots at speed is much easier with suspension.

● To negotiate big rocks, stay out of the saddle, keep your speed well down, and use your body to steer the bike around or over them, using some of the trick techniques which follow in the next section. If the rocks are wet and slimy, they may be super slippery, which will require a careful, balanced approach. Beware of crunching your chainwheels.

● left *Having the confidence to ride fast means knowing what surfaces to watch for and what techniques to employ to get over them. Practice at low speeds, and never ride fast on a track you don't know.*

The most useful tricks in the mountain-bike repertoire involve holding the bike still while lifting the front or back wheels to get them over an obstacle or to turn the bike in a tight radius. These tricks rely on timing, balance, self-confidence and control, and are worth practicing at every opportunity. They are much easier when performed with clipless pedals.

● right *Mountain bikes are a great cross between bikes that are very stable, and ones that allow you to do tricks. Here, John Tomac wheelies into first place.*

● right *Not the sort of thing that you need to do everyday, but car riding is possible on any mountain bike. Not something to try at home though!*

● opposite *Never mind not putting your feet on the table; don't put your bike on it either. Hans Rey shows us how to clear the table, in a quite different way.*

techniques – advanced riding

trackstand

This is a trick which has been highly developed by track racers, who balance on stationary bikes while they wait to see who will be first to make a move. It is useful on a mountain bike if you want to halt and briefly assess the situation, or make a change in direction by hopping the bike to one side.

The trackstand is best learned by riding the bike uphill on a slight slope. Let the bike come to a halt, and then adopt the following position with your feet clipped into the pedals:

- Rider standing up on the pedals with arms held straight
- Right pedal forward at about 30 degrees above the horizontal
- Handlebars turned at about 45 degrees to the right

A practiced rider should be able to hold this position for minutes at a time. Balance can be maintained by easing pressure off and on the right pedal to inch the bike backwards and forwards. It can be held on flat ground or on a moderately steep uphill, where the right foot is used to exert enough pressure to prevent the bike from sliding back. It cannot be held in a downhill position, since there is nothing to push the cranks against.

The trackstand can be useful for hopping the bike into a new position or direction. With your feet clipped into the pedals, small jumps can be used to hop the bike sideways or around in a circle, lifting the wheels a short distance off the ground each time, with the front wheel straightened during each hop. If the front wheel lifts more than the rear wheel, or vice versa, move your body position to compensate.

● right *Practice holding the bike in a trackstand somewhere safe off road. Pedal and handlebar control are everything.*

wheelies

All front-wheel lifts are based on the wheelie, in which the front wheel becomes airborne and the bike is balanced on the rear wheel. The basic technique is to pull up hard on the handlebars, driving the top pedal down, and throwing your weight back to lift the front wheel. The action of driving the pedal down also accelerates the bike forwards. If you want to wheelie in a confined space, just pull up on the bars and move your weight back to get the front wheel lifting.

The main use for a rear wheelie on the trail is usually to get over a rock or log which is barring your way. As soon as the front wheel drops down you must move your body forwards to lift the rear wheel so that it too can clear the obstruction. If you fail to do this in time, the rear wheel may hit the obstruction and stall the bike; if you do it too soon, the front wheel may crash into the obstruction and send you over the bars. If you are riding fast and put too much weight over the front as the rear wheel comes over the obstruction, you may also go over the bars. It is all a matter of judgment and timing.

● left and above *Sure, a wheelie can be used to clear a log or small step, but what the heck, these tricks are just great fun!*

● **far right** *Riding should become something that you enjoy. Try to get into a routine of going out every day for half an hour or so. Fitness soon builds up.*

● **opposite below** *Fitness means being able to get off the beaten track and enjoy yourself.*

● **below** *The kickturn is a BMX move that mountain bikers have hijacked to give them the ability to turn in very small spaces. It's useful on steep climbs, but done incorrectly can result in your looping out backwards.*

bunnyhops

The bunnyhop lifts both wheels into the air at the same time, allowing the rider to clear an obstruction. It can be practiced on flat ground at moderate speed. The technique is, first, to pre-load the jump by pushing down your body. A split second later lift the front wheel by pulling up on the bars, throwing your weight back, and jumping upright on the pedals with the cranks held level in a single dynamic movement. This lifts the rear wheel, as you pull your feet up under your body to give the wheel as much air as possible. The front wheel will touch down first, and the arms should be bent to soak up the impact before the rear wheel follows behind.

The bunnyhop can be modified into a sideways hop. This can be useful for getting

out of ruts, which only require a short hop sideways combined with a sufficiently high jump. The principles of lifting the bike into the air are the same, and the sideways movement is created by bending your upper body in the direction you want the bike to go, and then flicking your hips the same way in a single dynamic sideways movement. This will move the airborne wheels in a sideways drift beneath you before they touch down.

tight turns

Tight turns can be divided between the endo turn, which lifts the rear wheel, and the kick turn, which lifts the front wheel. The endo turn can be used to make a sudden change in direction on level ground or when riding downhill; the kick turn can be used for the same purpose on an uphill. Both turns can be used to spin the bike through 180 degrees.

To execute an endo turn, start to turn in the direction you want to go and then pull hard on the front brake. This will lift the rear wheel, while forward momentum combined with a push from your hips will make the bike turn as you balance on the front wheel, easing off the brake and stopping the hip movement as the rear wheel drops back down. Good brake control and body balance are required to avoid overdoing the rear-wheel lift, which could result in crashing over the bars.

A kick turn has a similar effect, but is executed by lifting the front wheel and spinning round while balanced on the rear wheel. Start to steer into the turn in the split second before you pull up on the bars and drive down the up-pedal to lift the bike in a powerful wheelie. Momentum and hip movement can again be used to guide the airborne front of the bike round to the direction you want to go. When riding uphill the kick turn is at its most useful for tight turns on singletrack, but take care to control the wheelies so that you do not flip over backwards on the rear wheel.

getting fit

Medical experts agree that cycling is an excellent means of building physical fitness. It is available to a wide range of people, with physical benefits that can be compared with running, swimming, walking, weight training, or a set of aerobics in a gym. In addition it can take you where you want to go surprisingly fast, and in the form of mountain biking has the advantage of getting you out into clean air, away from the poisonous fumes spewed out by traffic.

Cycling any kind of bike has many health benefits. It is a form of aerobic (cardiovascular) exercise which can help to prevent the build-up of clogged arteries, put your heart in better shape through tough exercise, and give you lower blood pressure with a slower heart beat when your body is at rest. It also promotes the flexibility of your body and builds muscular strength and endurance, without subjecting the joints and muscles of your lower body to such potentially damaging stress as jogging. The kind of recurrent injuries associated with contact sports are not a problem, and it is quite normal for cyclists to continue to ride hard into old age.

To outside observers there is another more obvious benefit of cycling, for as you twirl the pedals you burn up calories at the same time. How much this helps to control your body fat will depend on your metabolism, eating habits and level of exertion. The bottom line is that the harder you ride, the more you will burn. For instance, it has been estimated that a recreational rider averaging 10mph may burn 10 calories in a mile, while a racer averaging 30mph over the same distance may burn almost 60 calories. Either way, those who cycle regularly and energetically are usually people who eat well and stay slim.

diet and fitness

The most important energy supply on a hard ride comes from glycogen. This is a glucose product which is created by carbohydrates and is stored by your body ready for use by the muscles. The problem is that it is available only in a limited supply, after which slower-acting fat is called upon to power your muscles and less physical energy becomes available as exhaustion sets in. Lack of glycogen and the resulting need to slow down is known by long-distance runners as "hitting the wall."

You should not hit the wall unless you ride too long and too hard. If that is the kind of riding you want to do, pay particular attention to building up glycogen reserves. This can be achieved only with a controlled exercise programme coupled with a controlled diet. In the final count-down in the days before a particularly hard ride, the general idea is to increase your level of carbohydrates at the expense of fatty foods, while going easy on exercise in order to enable your body to store as much glycogen as possible. Carbohydrate foods to choose from include potatoes, rice, pasta, cereal, bread, and bananas, but carbohydrate-rich foods such as cakes and cheese which also contain high fat levels should be avoided. Be especially sure to eat well on the evening and morning before a long ride, allowing at least two hours for your low-fat, carbo-loaded breakfast to be digested.

food en-route

On any ride of more than two hours you should be prepared to take regular snacks and drinks. Specialized sports products such as "Power Bars" are easily carried and can give a good result, though more natural, cheaper foods such as bananas, dried apricots, and raisins perform just as well. Any snacks with a high fat content, such as chocolate crunch bars, are to be avoided as they are too slow-acting to produce energy quickly. Bulkier lunch foods such as sandwiches are best spread with jam or honey, rather than cheese or peanut butter, to give quick digestibility, and they should be washed down immediately with a drink.

If you finish a ride with another hard day ahead, you should start re-building glycogen levels while blood flow is still active through the muscles. You probably have no more than two hours before the muscles change down to their normal state, when they will accept only a much lower intake of glycogen, so you should aim to eat a carbohydrate-based snack without delay – or even a full plate of pasta if you can handle it.

● above *Energy powder is added to water to either top up your carbohydrate level, or to replace minerals and salts lost through sweat. Always follow the instructions, and use the product in training as well as racing.*

● right *There are a large number of energy bars on the market to help you increase your reserves while you're riding. They vary in flavor, so try a few and see what you think of the taste.*

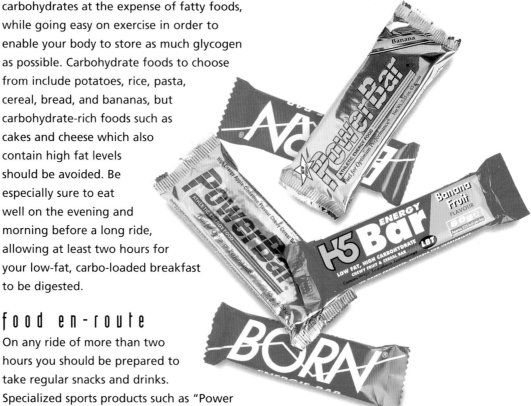

drink en-route

If you ride hard in hot conditions you can lose as much as 3½ pints of sweat in an hour. If you fail to replace it by taking a regular drink, dehydration can set in and the results are neither pleasant nor safe. As your body dries out your physical ability deteriorates, and if you allow things to get worse the symptoms can include an aching head, total exhaustion and possibly blurred vision. Only a suitably long period of rest and rehydration will overcome this.

If you wait until you feel you need a drink, it may be too late. If the weather is at all hot and you are riding hard, you should make a practice of taking a small drink from your water bottle or CamelBak every 15 minutes. Take particular care when riding at high altitude, when low humidity speeds evaporation from the skin – which may be wrongly interpreted as a lack of sweat.

The simplest and fastest method to stave off dehydration is to top up with water. For maximum performance this can be combined with a simple carbohydrate glucose polymer powder packaged as a "Sports Drink," which is rapidly absorbed by the stomach and helps maintain glucose levels for the muscles. If you are planning another hard ride the next day, a glucose polymer drink should also be taken immediately after the end of a ride to help speed recovery and top up the glycogen. Some of these sports drinks may not be very palatable, but ordinary sweet, carbohydrate-rich drinks should be avoided as they get into your bloodstream more slowly. Nor is alcohol a good idea when riding. Apart from the possibility of impairing your judgment, it is a diuretic – which means you will need to urinate more and so have to drink more to compensate.

goal-setting

To get cycling-fit and stay that way you should aim to get out regularly on your mountain bike. You can chart your progress and level of fitness by setting goals, steadily increasing your mileage and average speeds. If you want an accurate gauge of physical improvement, you can set up a fixed test course over known terrain for a fixed distance of around 4 to 6 miles. Always warm up your body for at least 10 minutes before you attempt to ride hard, and then ride the fixed course flat out to establish a base time. You can then return to the test once a month to gauge your progress.

If you are a serious biker, you should consider having a weekly program of rides. In summer you could plan for up to six daily sessions of one to two hours a day, allowing one day's total rest to combat boredom as well as physical overload. Depending on weather conditions and light availability, this will probably have to be cut back in the winter, when you could aim for two weekend rides of up to three hours coupled with a hard ride of at least one hour during the week if possible.

● above *Riding with friends in areas far off the beaten track is not only a great way to get fit, but is also a great thing to do. Ride to enjoy.*

● right *The heartrate monitor is a training aid which translates into optimum performance in a race.*

When your heart and lungs are unable to supply sufficient oxygen to the muscles, blood lactate is produced, which causes the muscles to tire – with fatigue increasing as the exercise gets harder. So the next stage may be to invest in a heart rate monitor or pulsometer, which gives you an instant handlebar read-out as you pedal along. To use it effectively you will need to know your threshold heart rate, which is an approximation of how fast your heart beats when riding flat out over a fixed distance for about 20 minutes. You can then train to the four main levels used by professional cyclists to improve heart condition, oxygen supply and aerobic levels:

Level 1: Heart rate is 20–30 beats below threshold rate. This involves a long, steady ride, up to four hours in duration, which requires no great effort. Aim to do one or two rides per week at this level.

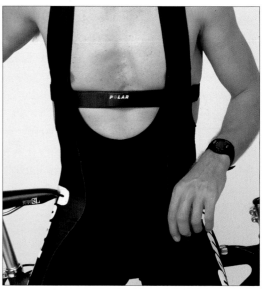

Level 2: Heart rate is 10–15 beats below threshold rate. This is likely to be a fairly fast ride lasting not much longer than an hour. During the ride you are breathing steadily and hard and only minimal conversation is possible. Aim for one or two rides a week at this level.

Level 3: Heart rate is close to threshold rate. This is characterised by intense riding with rapid breathing, with no chance of conversation and maximum aerobic effort over a period of about 30 minutes. Aim for one ride a week at this level.

Level 4: Heart rate is above threshold rate. This is a short burst of high-intensity riding for little more than one minute, which puts maximum load on the cardiovascular system. It can be repeated several times in a session, with interval rests of around five minutes. Aim for one ride a week at this level.

maintaining your equipment

Mountain-bike maintenance is a major subject which is only touched on in this chapter. It is dealt with in detail by a number of good books specifically devoted to looking after your bike. With time and patience anyone who likes fiddling with mechanical things and is willing to buy the necessary tools should be able to give a mountain bike virtually all the maintenance it will need. If you run into trouble there is always a friendly repair shop waiting to help you for a modest price.

Many riders prefer to keep time spent on riding to a maximum and time spent on maintenance to a minimum. Nevertheless they should always be prepared to check on the performance and safety of their bikes, and know when it is time to ask a professional to sort out upcoming problems.

regular checks

Give your bike a comprehensive check-up and service on a regular basis. How often you need to do this will depend on how hard and how often you ride, and what the conditions are. For instance, a bike that is frequently ridden through mud will build up different maintenance problems from a bike which spends its time on hard, dry tracks. The main requirement is to be aware of the condition of your bike, and deal with any potential problems before they occur.

● Adjust your brakes and, if necessary, replace the blocks. Strip, clean, and lubricate the cantilever mechanisms annually.

● Check cables for fraying and damage, and clean and lubricate if necessary. A cable is unlikely to break, but if the housings get full of dirt, gear changing becomes unresponsive. Change cables and housings annually.

● Keep the front and rear derailleur mechanisms clean, and check that side-to-side travel and cable length are correct for perfect changing. Check that the rear derailleur arm has not been bent out of true owing to an impact. (It is designed to bend rather than break, and with care it can usually be pulled back into alignment.)

● Check that the chain runs smoothly, with no links sticking. If the chain is dirty, give it a bath in a chain cleaner. If there are signs of rust, it needs lubrication. Check the chain for signs of wear and stretch. If it looks in poor condition, replace it before it starts to chew off the teeth of the sprockets and chainrings. Replace it annually as a matter of course.

● Check the teeth of the chainrings. Check that the crank arms are tight on the axle, and that the pedals are tight on the cranks. Check for any play in the bottom bracket, which should turn smoothly. Check for any play in the pedals, which should spin almost silently.

● Check that the wheel hubs run free. They too should spin almost silently. If the wheel moves from side to side, the cones are loose and will need adjusting. Check that the freewheel runs free and is clean and well lubricated.

● Check that the headset is tight enough to hold the forks securely, without being too stiff when turning the bars.

● left *This chain bath is ideal for maintaining an efficient chain.*

• The bottom bracket, front and rear hubs, headset, and pedals should ideally be dismantled, cleaned, and re-greased on a regular basis. How frequent this is will depend on how hard and how frequently they have been used, how effective the seals are at keeping out dirt and water, and how suitable the units are for stripping and rebuilding rather than replacement.

• Check the tires for wear, tear, and pressure, and remove anything stuck between the treads. If you have a slow puncture, repair or replace the tube. You should consider replacing tires and inner tubes annually. Check that the wheels are true, with even spoke tension. Carefully check the rims to ensure there is no damage which could lead to a split in the aluminum.

• If your bike has clipless pedals, replace the cleats on your shoes every year.

• If your bike has suspension, check the elastomers or air/oil units according to the manufacturer's recommendation. Hydraulic brake systems should also be lubricated and serviced as recommended.

frame damage

If you are the type of easygoing rider who prefers smooth tracks and trails, the frame and forks of a good-quality bike should give many years of trouble-free service. You should nevertheless inspect the frame and forks on a regular basis, filling in chipped paintwork and removing any rust spots.

If you are the kind of rider who blasts down rocky hillsides, throws the bike through powerful turns and gets plenty of air under the wheels, the frame of your bike will take a battering and have a finite life. In the hands of a hard-riding professional racer this will not extend beyond a single season. If you fall into the hard-riding category, you should make a regular check of your frame and forks to guard against the possibility of major structural failure. Aluminium mountain bikes are theoretically most likely to fail, though carbon, steel and titanium may also be vulnerable. Check your bike carefully every time you wash it, removing the wheels so that you can give it a full inspection. Look at all the potential weak spots, such as the

• left *Some things can't be avoided, and when this rider hit a rock at nearly 50mph, a destroyed rear wheel was the result.*

technique — advanced riding

bottom bracket and head-tube junctions; the top of the seat tube, where stress is caused by the seatpost; and the drop-outs, in particular the rear drop-out area, where the chain can rub on the inside. If there is any sign of a crack forming, do not ride the bike before seeking expert advice.

cleaning a bike

Mountain bikes get dirty, and dirt and performance to not go together well. Ideally you should clean your bike after every ride. This may range from wiping off a light coating of dust to hosing and washing off a thick layer of congealed mud. If you leave it, the dirt builds up, the performance deteriorates, the group-set wears out faster than it should, and you will eventually be faced by a major clean-up operation with the possibility of having to replace worn parts.

All the moving parts of the bike need to be lubricated. Perhaps the greatest skill required in cleaning a bike is learning how to avoid spreading grease and accompanying grime which will stick to any surface it can find. The first rule is to keep your hands as clean as possible throughout the cleaning procedure.

● Hose off any mud while it is still wet and easy to remove. The higher the hose pressure, the easier it will be to clean the bike. But bear in mind that high-pressure water will also wash lubrication out of the bearings. So make a point of giving your bike a thorough lubrication inspection after any high-pressure hosing, and avoid blasting bearing seals directly.

● Use a proprietary degreaser to clean the sprockets, rear derailleur jockey wheels and derailleur mechanism, chain, chainwheels and front derailleur mechanism, using a brush to apply it. Use a stiff bristle brush if required, plus a purpose-designed, rigid-plastic freewheel brush to get between the sprockets.

● Use a sponge and a car-wash detergent, preferably with warm water, to clean the frame.

● Use the same water with a hard brush to clean the inaccessible areas around the brake cantilevers, brake and gear levers, wheel rims, pedals, hubs, bottom bracket, inside the chainwheels and under the saddle.

● Hose off the degreaser or wash it off with a sponge and cold water. To remove excess grease from the chain you can wipe it with an old cloth. If the chain is still dirty, you can run it through a proprietary chain bath or remove it and leave it to soak in a jar filled with degreaser.

● Polish the frame with a metal cleaner or spray wax, which will remove any remaining stains as well as leaving a shiny finish.

● Make sure the bike is fully dry before you start lubricating.

● *above* **Keep your bike well maintained, then you'll easily be able to see if there's anything wrong with it. Take care not to blast the bearings with water or the grease will be forced out.**

lubricating a bike

There is a confusing mass of products available for lubricating a mountain bike, many of which are attractively packaged with eye-popping price tags that are a world away from a humble can of oil.

The most widely favoured products are medium-weight lubricants which are synthetic and water resistant; many incorporate PTFE or Teflon, which makes the lubricant cleaner and easier to handle. They are most easily applied to the chain drop by drop, which is slow but accurate, or they are sprayed onto sprockets and derailleur mechanisms, which is fast but less precise. Excess lubricant should be wiped off, and the remaining lubricant allowed to dry before you ride the bike.

A heavy-duty mountain-bike grease should be used to re-lubricate the bearings in the headset, bottom brackets, wheel hubs, pedals and suspension units when required. It can also be used to lubricate the seatpost and stem to prevent them jamming. This same grease can be used to lubricate brake (but not gear) cables as they pass through their housings. A lightweight, water-resistant lubricant such as WD-40 completes the line-up and is useful for spraying on gear cables, pivot points such as brake levers and cantilevers and as general external protection for clipless pedals.

tools and home workshop

The minimum requirements for a comprehensive home workshop will include most of the following:

● Workstand. The bike should ideally be rigidly supported with both wheels lifted clear of the ground. The best models are infinitely adjustable; cheaper models lift the rear wheel only, which is useful for adjusting the derailleurs.

● Tool storage. To store tools use either a marked-out toolboard on the wall, conventional toolbox, magnetic kitchen rack or a purpose-designed product such as the Park Tool Caddy.

● below *Invest in good quality tools such as these double ended Park spanners.*

● right *You will also need one high quality 6-inch adjustable wrench.*

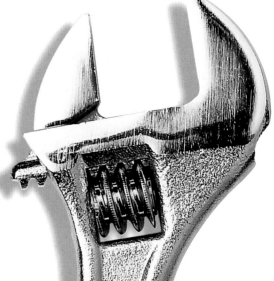

● Basic tools. Tire levers (two or three, depending on how tight your tires are on the rims); allen or hex keys covering the 2–6mm size range; small adjustable wrench; ring wrenches from 8-17mm; 13/14mm or 15/16mm cone wrenches (2) which must be narrow enough to fit against each other; pliers; small-size standard and Phillips screwdrivers; chain-breaker for breaking and re-joining links; chain bath for washing the chain; spoke key for tuning the spokes; crank extractor to remove the chainwheels (it must be the correct size for your model); cable cutter for replacing cables; headset wrenches (2) in the correct sizes for headset lubrication and adjustment; grease gun for pumping in grease; track pump with pressure gauge.

● a b o v e *Chain lifter*

Pin spanners

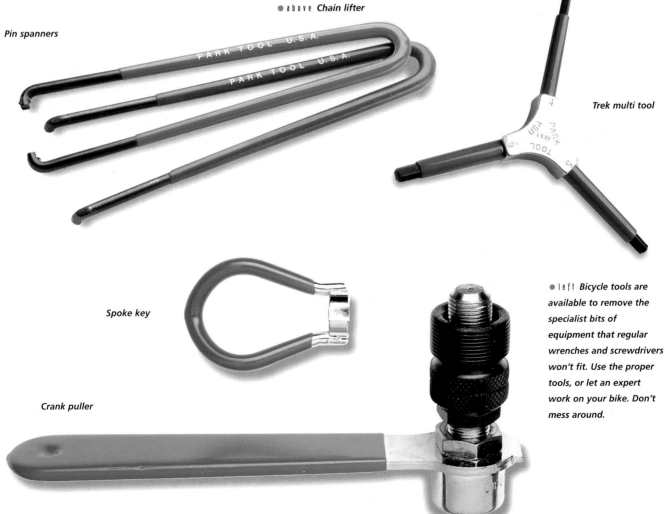

Trek multi tool

Spoke key

Crank puller

● l e f t *Bicycle tools are available to remove the specialist bits of equipment that regular wrenches and screwdrivers won't fit. Use the proper tools, or let an expert work on your bike. Don't mess around.*

6 mountain bike competition

cross-country

Cross-country is the principal discipline in mountain-bike racing, and usually the toughest. After a massed start, competitors race around a clearly marked course and the first rider to cross the finish line is the winner. The course can be up to 10 miles in length or even longer, with the number of laps determining the total length of the race. A professional Grundig Series event is likely to be around 30 miles long, taking the winner over two hours to complete, while local amateur events will be considerably shorter.

● below *The start of a cross country race is a frantic affair with everyone jostling for positions.*

Cross-country racing is a mass-participation sport which requires intense individual effort. There is little opportunity for the kind of team tactics that are used in a road race, and no slipstreaming or cruising while waiting for someone to make a break. The fastest riders usually hit the front of the field as soon as they can and stay there, not least because overtaking can be difficult and dangerous on singletrack or technical descents. The course should be designed to provide a testing mixture of terrain, including plenty of hard climbing and fast downhills, and in wet weather lack of traction may force riders to dismount and run with their bikes in cyclo-cross fashion, which can make a race particularly gruelling. Crashes are not unusual, although there are few serious injuries; punctures are an ever-present hazard, which can suddenly stop a rider at the front or back of the field. No outside help is permitted, and top professional riders are so skilled that they have been known to change a flat in little more than a minute.

The bikes used for cross-country are little different from the high-performance stock bikes marketed for general off-road use. Those used by top professionals may be a little lighter and made-to-measure for the

● left *A good climb soon starts to sort the field out.*

mountain bike competition

● left *The start of a major event such as a Grundig World Cup series, puts competitors under maximum pressure to perform for their sponsors.*

rider's height and reach, and will almost certainly feature top group-sets. Clipless pedals are standard issue, and virtually all riders now use front suspension units, which are generally much faster on downhills. Adoption of full suspension has been slow among top riders, although three-time World Champion Hendrik Djernis opted to change to the all-suspension Pro-Flex team at the start of the 1995 season.

downhill

Racing downhill at high speeds is potentially the most dangerous form of mountain-bike competition, and downhill is primarily staged as an off-road time-trial discipline. Riders start at intervals, and whoever records the fastest time from top to bottom of the course is the winner. Despite its simple nature it is a discipline which requires a very positive mental approach, which includes knowing your limits, a high level of physical fitness, superb bike-handling skills, and the ability to read the course at high speeds and set the

● left *Once you're on the course, it's like riding by yourself, except you have other riders chasing you. This is Rune Hoydahl.*

competition mountain bike

bike up for each bend. Maintaining control is the vital ingredient for winning.

The downhill course used at Vail, Colorado, for the 1994 Mountain Bike World Championship was typical of the highly demanding courses set for top professionals. Starting at an altitude of 10,250ft, it dropped 2,000ft over 2¾ miles, combining high-speed open sections, technical singletrack through winding woodland, and tight turns. The winner, François Gachet, took 6 minutes 22.52 seconds to cover the course in the finals. Gachet was also World Downhill Champion in 1993, and won the Grundig/UCI Downhill World Cup series in both 1993 and 1994.

In general terms a conventional bike can be successfully used for amateur downhill. However, a more upright position is favored than for cross-country, for good forward vision and precise control, with the saddle dropped down to keep the center of gravity low for fast cornering and wide handlebars fitted. Brake systems can be

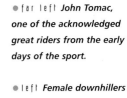

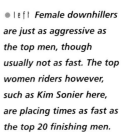

● far left *John Tomac, one of the acknowledged great riders from the early days of the sport.*

● left *Female downhillers are just as aggressive as the top men, though usually not as fast. The top women riders however, such as Kim Sonier here, are placing times as fast as the top 20 finishing men.*

mountain bike competition

uprated to more powerful hydraulics; wide tires with maximum traction are preferred; and a device such as a DCD will prevent the chain bouncing off the outer chainring at speed.

At the top of the sport a bike for downhill is likely to be a much more dedicated beast, which is heavily modified or specially built for the purpose of going very fast and staying in control on a downhill. For instance, François Gachet's custom-built 1994 World Championship bike had a relatively long wheelbase at 3ft 9in to maximize control, and weighed over 34lb, which illustrates that a strong bike which will withstand a real hammering is much more important than the light weight which is needed to help a cross-country bike uphill.

Full suspension is mandatory to cope with the lumps and bumps on most downhill courses. Gachet's bike featured 3in of suspension travel provided by air/oil shocks at the front and 4in of travel provided by a single spring coil mounted on a pivoting swing-arm at the rear. Gachet used a single, oversize 48-tooth chainring combined with an 8-speed 12x30 rear-sprocket cluster activated by a GripShift shifter to ensure he could sprint through the sections where his speed eased off. His chain was held firmly on the chainring by being fed through a jockey-wheel cage just below and behind the chainring, with a plastic chain guide at the top. His stopping power was provided by a hydraulic disc brake at the rear with a conventional cantilever brake at the front, though many downhillers now opt for front-wheel disc brakes.

For serious downhill use some riders wear full body armor, although a rider such as John Tomac prefers to wear little more than an aerodynamic skater's skinsuit, with a full-face helmet as the only concession to extra protection. Shin and knee pads, goggles and gloves are also widely used by the top riders.

152

downhill variations

One problem with downhill is that there is no direct competition element to interest spectators since each rider is racing against the clock. To compensate for this, some race organizers run downhill events in which two racers set off together, with the first to the finish being the winner and heats held on a knock-out basis which culminates in the finals.

The most popular variation is downhill dual slalom, a discipline that is based on snow-skiing dual slalom. Two riders set off together to head down parallel courses marked by gates, weaving their way down around the left- and right-turn flags to the finish at the bottom. This requires a short, steep hill which is wide enough to give two competitors virtually identical terrain all the way down.

A downhill refinement which seems set to grow in popularity is the head-to-head downhill, a discipline which was pioneered by the 1993 Reebok Eliminator at Mammoth, in California. This event was designed specifically for TV coverage, with competitors racing man-to-man down a course based on

the world- famous Kamikaze, starting at 11,000ft and dropping to 2,150ft in 3½ miles. The paired riders were allowed two races down the course, with the winner decided on combined times, though there was a maximum 5 second time penalty in each race to ensure that crashing on one run would not necessarily mean elimination. To ensure that riders raced all the way down the course, the first rider to the halfway stage got a cash prize.

The ultimate downhill variation must be the quest for the Mountain Bike World Speed Record. In 1995 this was unofficially set at 111.04mph by the Frenchman Christian Taileffer during the Diesel Speed Challenge held at Vars in the French Alps. The course used a high-speed ski run, dropping at 45 degrees from a height of 1,090yd entering the measured kilometer, which dropped to 7,497ft at the finish, where average speeds were recorded, with a 1 kilometer (1,090yd) run-out ending in a slight uphill. The only woman entrant, Giovanna Bonazzi of Italy, recorded a speed of 88.63mph! All the competitors wore speed skiers' suits with

● opposite *Downhill racing is growing fast in popularity. The high-speed thrills are often proving much more attractive to sponsorship than the slower cross-country races.*

● left *Dual Slalom is one of the most exciting new developments in mountain biking. Deriving from ski-slalom, two riders race a head-to-head knockout formula with heats leading to finals to decide a winner. It's full of crashes, and the crowds love it.*

aerodynamic helmets, had 70-tooth chainrings to accelerate away from the start, and used spiked tires to grip the hard-packed snow.

Hillclimbs, of course, are the opposite of downhill events. Owing to the low speeds involved hillclimbs can be run as time trials or massed-start events, but for most spectators they lack the excitement of cross-country and downhill racing. By definition a hillclimb is an extremely tough event. As the popularity of downhill has increased, that of hillclimbing has rapidly declined since the early days of mountain-bike competition, when it was a major discipline at international events.

● above *Reaching the finish line at the end of a multi-lap race is a relief for many riders.*

competition categories

With big entries at mountain-bike events, cross-country and downhill competitors are often divided into age groups, which are listed by the UCI (Union Cycliste Internationale), the French-based governing body of all cycle sport including mountain biking as follows:

Fun/Novice: 10–12 years old.
Youth: 12 years old to the end of the year of your 16th birthday.
Junior: From the beginning of the year of your 17th birthday to the end of the year of your 18th birthday.

Senior: From the beginning of the year of your 19th birthday to the end of the year of your 34th birthday.
Veteran: From the beginning of the year of your 35th birthday to the end of the year of your 44th birthday.
Master: From the beginning of the year of your 45th birthday to the end of the year of your 54th birthday.
Super Master: From the beginning of the year of your 55th birthday and onwards.

Senior is the most popular and competitive age range at mountain-bike events, and is divided into four ability levels:
Pro/Elite: The top group of riders at any event, led by full-time professionals.
Expert: Experienced, very fit amateur riders who take the sport seriously. They may have progressed from Junior level and many will hope to move up to the Pro/Elite group.
Sport: Riders who are there to enjoy the racing, without being totally dedicated to the sport. *Sport 1* is for the 18–27 year-old age group; *Sport 2* for the 27–35 year-old age group.

the major events

The mountain bike professional season is dominated by the Grundig World Cup series and the annual World Championships; the first cross-country Olympics is to be staged in 1996. The modern World Cup came into being in 1991 when the European Grundig series combined with the American NORBA series in collaboration with the UCI. It is targeted for global appeal with as many as 10 events held each year in Australia, the United States and western and eastern Europe. At every event cross-country is the major discipline, with a shorter series of Grundig/UCI World Downhill Cup events held at the same time if the venues are suitable.

The World Cup series winner is decided on points amassed throughout the season, but the single big event that all pros want to win is the World Championship. This has been held at venues in Europe and the United

States since 1990. The disciplines are cross-country and downhill, with most interest in the Senior Men's and Women's classes. However, it can be a big event – at the 1994 World's at Vail in the United States there were also classes for Juniors and Veterans plus an unofficial Dual Slalom world championship, which produced a 900-strong entry from 44 countries, and attracted some 30,000 spectators. This was followed by the 1995 World Championship at Kirchzarten, near Freiburg, in the Black Forest region of Germany, staged on a 2.9-mile downhill course and the 5.3 mile Bickenreut cross-country circuit which climbed 935ft per lap.

The most famous international venue of all is Mammoth in California. Located some 300 miles north of Los Angeles, this was the site of the American-organized world Championships from 1987 to 1989. It features the legendary Kamikaze downhill course, starting from an altitude of 11,000 feet at the top of Mammoth Mountain. During the 1994 Grundig World Cup series the Mammoth event was a festival of cycle racing, attracting over 3,000 starters in 18 different events over a five-day period. This included 500 beginners entered in their own cross-country event, while a total of 180 Dual Slalom and Reebok Eliminator rounds took place.

world championships winners

1990 Durango, Colorado, U.S.A.
Senior Cross-Country, Men: **1.** Ned Overend (USA); **2.** Thomas Frischknecht (Switzerland); **3.** Tim Gould (U.K.).
Senior Cross-Country, Women: **1.** Julie Furtado (U.S.A.); **2.** Sara Ballantyne (U.S.A.); **3.** Ruthie Matthes (U.S.A.).
Senior Downhill, Men: **1.** Greg Herbold (U.S.A.); **2.** Mike Kloser (U.S.A.); **3.** Paul Thomasberg (U.S.A.).
Senior Downhill, Women: 1. Cindy Devine

(U.S.A.); 2. Elladee Brown (Canada); 3. Penny Davidson (U.S.A.).
1991 Lucca, Italy
Senior Cross-Country, Men: 1. John Tomac (U.S.A.); 2. Thomas Frischknecht (Switzerland); 3. Ned Overend (U.S.A.).
Senior Cross-Country, Women: 1. Ruthie Matthes (U.S.A.); 2. Eva Orvosova (Slovakia); 3. Silvia Furst (Switzerland).
Senior Downhill, Men: 1. Albert Iten (Switzerland); 2. John Tomac (U.S.A.); 3. Glen Adams (U.S.A.).
Senior Downhill, Women: 1. Giovanna Bonazzi (Italy); 2. Nathalie Fiat (France); 3.

● above *Season-long competitions give a chance for reliability to be an issue for the racers, but the World Championships is still the premier event.*

Cindy Devine (Canada).

1992 Bromont, Quebec, Canada
Senior Cross-Country, Men: 1. Henrik Djernis (Denmark); 2. Thomas Frischknecht (Switzerland); 3. Dave Baker (U.K.).
Senior Cross-Country, Women: 1. Silvia Furst (Switzerland); 2. Alison Sydor (Canada); 3. Ruthie Matthes (U.S.A.).
Senior Downhill, Men: 1. Dave Cullinan (U.S.A.); 2. Jimmy Deaton (U.S.A.); 3. Christian Taileffer (France).
Senior Downhill, Women: 1. Julie Furtado (U.S.A.); 2. Kim Sonier (U.S.A.); 3. Cindy Devine (Canada).

1993 Métabief, France
Senior Cross-Country, Men: 1. Henrik Djernis (Denmark); 2. Marcel Gerritsen (Holland); 3. Jan Ostergaard (Denmark).
Senior Cross-Country, Women: 1. Paola Pezzo (Italy); 2. Jeannie Longo (France); 3. Ruthie Matthes (U.S.A.).
Senior Downhill, Men: 1. Mike King (U.S.A.); 2. Paolo Caramellino (Italy); 3. Myles Rockwell (U.S.A.).
Senior Downhill, Women: 1. Giovanna Bonazzi (Italy); 2. Kim Sonier (U.S.A.); 3. Missy Giove (U.S.A.).

1994 Vail, Colorado, United States
Senior Cross-Country, Men: 1. Henrik Djernis (Denmark); 2. Tinker Juarez (U.S.A.); 3. Bart Brentjens (Holland).
Senior Cross-Country, Women: 1. Alison Sydor (U.S.A.); 2. Susan DeMattei (U.S.A.); 3. Sara Ballantyne (U.S.A.).
Senior Downhill, Men: 1. François Gachet (France); 2. Tommy Johansson (Sweden); 3. Corado Herin (Italy).
Senior Downhill, Women: 1. Missy Giove (U.S.A.); 2. Sophie Kempf (France); 3. Giovanna Bonazzi (Italy).

1995 Kirchzarten, Germany
Senior Cross-Country, Men: 1. Bart Brentjens (Holland); 2. Miguel Martinez (France); 3. Jan-Erik Ostergaard (Denmark).
Senior Cross-Country, Women: 1. Alison Sydor (Canada); 2. Silvia Fürst (Switzerland);

3. Chantal Daucourt (France).
Senior Downhill, Men: 1. Nicolas Vouilloz (France); 2. François Gachet (France); 3. Mike King (U.S.A.).
Senior Downhill, Women: 1. Leigh Donovan (U.S.A.); 2. Mercedes Gonzales (Spain); 3. Giovanna Bonazzi (Italy).

stage racing

Long distance cross-country stage racing is growing in interest and may be of major importance in years to come. In 1995 the world famous Tour de France road race organizers launched the first mountain-bike Tour de France known as the Tour VTT (Velo Tour Terrain – the French term for a mountain-bike). The nine-day event was contested by 20 teams, each consisting of five senior men and one woman. It was held on the same daily-stage principles as the Tour de France, with the racers and support teams housed in a huge tented village which moved with the event. After an opening off-road prologue, each day was divided into timed stages and untimed linking stages. This gave a total ride distance of 335 miles over a mountainous landscape between the start at Métabief (site of the 1993 World Championships and 1994 European Championships) and the finish at Le Bourboule, south-west of Clermont Ferrand, with a 1 million franc prize fund.

In Australia the 1995 Crocodile Trophy was billed as "the longest and most difficult mountain-bike stage race in the world," held over 1,585 miles between Darwin (Northern Territory) and Cairns (Queensland), with average daily stages of 93 miles. It started in the Kakadu National Park, with most of the route over bush tracks, across mountains, through tropical rainforests, and across unbridged rivers well stocked with crocodiles – hence the name of the race. It was staged as an open event for both professionals and amateurs, with a tented camp following the race to provide full back up.

other competitive events

Observed trials are based on a popular discipline in off-road motorcycle sport. An event is decided on a series of technical sections which are designed to be extremely difficult to ride. Speed is not a winning element, although there may be a time limit. The competition is likely to be decided on how many times each competitor puts a foot down or grasps something to retain his balance. Points are added on for every such incident, and the rider with the lowest total wins overall. Owing to their technical difficulty and lack of any high-speed excitement, trials tend to be a minority interest.

Enduro is more of a long-distance event which combines trials with a cross-country course. Riders win on a combination of technical riding skills on the special stages, speed over the ground between the stages, and map-reading skills to find their way around the course. Trailquest combines orienteering with mountain biking, and places high emphasis on navigation. A refinement is a two-day event, such as the Polaris Challenge held in Britain. Teams sleep out overnight while finding their way between checkpoints in wilderness country, carrying all the necessary survival equipment on their bodies and bikes.

● above *Ned Overend has been racing mountain bikes for as long as mountain bikes have been racing. He's considered one of the greatest riders in the world, despite being the oldest top-level Pro rider.*

Numbers in *italics* refer to illustrations

index

index

index